BECOMING
GOD'S PEOPLE TODAY

The Church's Mission in an Urban World

by Alice and Willard Roth

HERALD PRESS, SCOTTDALE, PENNSYLVANIA

FAITH AND LIFE PRESS, NEWTON, KANSAS

1

CREDITS

Cover design by Joe Alderfer

"Our World Is God's World" (pages 6-11) is adapted from a
brochure written by Harvey G. Cox for the American Baptist
Home Mission Societies, Valley Forge, Pa.; used by permission.

"Love and You Will Live" (page 23) is extracted from "Who
Is My Neighbor?" by Virgil Vogt in Gospel Herald, Aug.
25, 1959.

Old Testament references and the references from Acts 2 in
chapter 10 are from the Revised Standard Version, copyright 1946 and 1952 by the Division of Christian Education,
National Council of Churches; used by permission.

New Testament references are from The New English Bible,
copyright 1961 by the Delegates of the Oxford University
Press and the Syndics of the Cambridge University Press;
used by permission.

Photographs: Pages 7, 8, 11, 66, 95, Edward Wallowitch;
32, Calvin L. Miller; 34, Orville Andrews; 44, 76, 86, 108,
Paul M. Schrock; 48, Central Feature News; 56, H. Arm-
strong Roberts; 98, Mennonite Community Association;
120, Neil Baumgarten, Eastman Kodak Scholastic Award
Winner; 132, S. F. Pannabecker, courtesy Mennonite Biblical
Seminary.

BECOMING GOD'S PEOPLE TODAY

Foreword

ONCE long ago a Man stood above a city and wept. Many times since, other men have looked at the city from a comfortably detached distance, gazed upon its neon lights, cursed its darkness, wept--then turned to go another way. But the first Man wiped His tears, walked down the hill toward the heart of the city. He calculated the risk, and accepted it. He counted the cost, and paid it. Because of what He did, His followers can live in the city with expectant hope. "On the holy mount stands the city he founded; the Lord loves the gates of Zion more than all the dwelling places of Jacob. Glorious things are spoken of you, O city of God" (Psalm 87:1-3).

"The reason we fly from the city," G. K. Chesterton has said, "is not that it is not poetical; it is that its poetry is too fierce, too fascinating, and too practical in its demands." But the company who follows the Man must, like Him, walk toward the heart of the fierce, but fascinating city. We recognize with gratitude, then, that the world in which God has called His people to live and to love in the latter years of century twenty is the world of the city.

So we aim in this study to consider together what it means to be Christian in a world that is increasingly urban. We write not as theologians, nor as sociologists, nor even as practicing urban churchmen, but as journalists involved in Christian mission. While our words are tentative, we hope they are not tottering. We mean what we write to be serious but not dogmatic. What we here set forth we trust may lead from deliberate discussion toward responsible *being* and *doing* and *speaking*. In short, toward becoming God's people today.

Contents

For Reflection

For Study

FOR REFLECTION

Our World Is God's World

Our world
Is a place where people are born,
Where they work and marry and shop for groceries,
Where they laugh and suffer and die.

Some live for worthwhile purposes,
Some for petty ends,
Some seem to live for no reason at all.

What is this world of ours
With its endless parade of people and events?
Is there any purpose to it, any meaning?
Where is it going?
Christians say, "Our world is God's world."

God lives and works in our world,
Not in some far-off galaxy,
Not in some ethereal, ideal world,
Not just when human life is over,
Not merely in "religious activities."
Our world is God's world.

In our work and play,
In our singing and crying,
In our building . . . even in our destroying,
In our living and dying,
God works out His purposes for us.
Sometimes secretly, sometimes openly;
Sometimes thwarted, yet eventually victorious;
God works in our world,
Reconciling men to each other, and to Himself.

Most openly of all, God worked in the life of one Man.

In Jesus, men saw God at work in the world.

Jesus brought
Wholeness to the palsied in body and spirit,
Liberty to the victims of captivity and racial conceit,
Healing to those sick with fear and emptiness.
In Him men saw more clearly than they ever had
That God was at work in their midst.
Yet men have always found God's love too much to bear,

For their secret hatred and greed have been exposed by His love.
When Jesus died on the cross,
Men believed God had gone forever from human life.

"And there was darkness over the whole earth. . . . "

Yet God's stake in human destiny
Was too great to be destroyed by death.
God did not forsake men.
Something wonderful happened,
For Jesus' defeated and scattered followers
Joyously spoke of a living Lord,
Of a new spirit in their midst,
Of a promise that He would never leave them.
God was not driven out of human life.
He is still at work . . . healing, restoring, reconciling.
Now men know He will never leave human history.
They know He will accomplish His purpose.
Men know they can live at peace with other men
And spend their lives in careless disregard for self.

In the risen Lord, God is present
In human life for eternity.

Still men must be told
Our world is God's world;
So God has a people whose work it is to tell the news,
A people called "the church."

These people are just like any other people.
They are born, they work,
They marry, they shop for groceries,
They die.

Yet they believe the world they live in is God's world,
That God works in it the way He worked in Jesus . . .
Healing, restoring, reconciling.
And somehow, this belief makes all the difference.

God's people have a job to do for Him:
To tell men that our world is God's world,
To show them that what God did in Jesus
He continues to do.

God's people often fail.
But He calls them back to Him;
They confess their failings,
And He forgives them and makes them strong
To be His people in the world again.

God's people want others to find Him, to know
Him in Jesus . . . in the cup and the bread in the world.
God's people want others to find Him, to know.

They want all men to know the great news
That our world belongs to God.

Some have never heard that God has chosen
Every man to be His child.
The church's doors open outward;
So God's people go out
To be about their Father's business.

Chosen to Be a People

"'For you are a people holy to the Lord your God; the Lord your God has chosen you to be a people for his own possession, out of all the peoples that are on the face of the earth. It was not because you were more in number than any other people that the Lord set his love upon you and chose you, you were the fewest of all peoples; but it is because the Lord loves you, and is keeping the oath which he swore to your fathers, that the Lord has brought you out with a mighty hand, and redeemed you from the house of bondage, from the hand of Pharaoh king of Egypt. Know therefore that the Lord your God is God, the faithful God who keeps covenant and steadfast love with those who love him and keep his commandments, to a thousand generations, and requites to their face those who hate him, by destroying them; he will not be slack with him who hates him, he will requite him to his face. You shall therefore be careful to do the commandment, and the statutes, and the ordinances, which I command you this day'" (Deuteronomy 7:6-11).

"But you are a chosen race, a royal priesthood, a dedicated nation, and a people claimed by God for his own, to proclaim the triumphs of him who has called you out of darkness into his marvellous light. You are now the people of God, who once were not his people; outside his mercy once, you have now received his mercy" (I Peter 2:9, 10).

God moved first. But then God chose to continue His work in the world which He created through people whom He Himself would choose. The work which God wants done--or to put it another way, the mission of His chosen people--is to tell all men that God loves them; to invite all men to love God and to live His way; to proclaim triumphantly that life with God is rich with meaning.

The Old Testament reports the beginning of the story of "the faithful God who keeps covenant and steadfast love with those who love him and keep his commandments." Covenant means agreement--an agreement in which each side is tied to undertakings on the other's behalf. The covenant referred to throughout the Scripture began with God's desire to enter into partnership with men. Covenant then denotes a gracious undertaking by God to benefit and bless those men of faith who commit themselves to the obligations which this undertaking involves.

After an extensive prologue, the Biblical story narrows down to the wanderings of Abraham--the man to whom God said, "Behold, my covenant is with you, and you shall be the father of a multitude of nations" (Genesis 17:4). Abraham moved from Ur, to Haran, and on into Palestine where two generations of his descendants (the Hebrew people) were born and lived. Then, in a time of famine, they went to Egypt. While in Egypt God commissioned Moses to lead the Hebrews out through the wilderness of Sinai and finally back into Palestine, the land of their forefathers. King Pharaoh, wanting to hold on to his cheap labor, pursued the Hebrews but God miraculously helped His people out of bondage. After 40 years in the wilderness Moses speaks to Israel--he recounts their wanderings, reviews the Ten Commandments, interprets the great commandment, and continues with the words recorded in Deuteronomy 7:6-11.

Moses explains that their Exodus from Egypt marked their identity as a nation. As an experience of God's grace, the Exodus defined the nature of the God with whom they had to do--a God of loving concern. He chose His people, not because of any superiority or merit of theirs, but out of sheer love.

13

We Are the People

"Paul rose, made a gesture with his hand, and began:

"Men of Israel and you who worship our God, listen to me! The God of this people of Israel chose our fathers. When they were still living as aliens in Egypt he made them into a nation and brought them out of that country with arm outstretched. For some forty years he bore with their conduct in the desert. Then in the Canaanite country he overthrew seven nations, whose lands he gave them to be their heritage for some four hundred and fifty years, and afterwards appointed judges for them until the time of the prophet Samuel.

"Then they asked for a king and God gave them Saul the son of Kish, a man of the tribe of Benjamin, who reigned for forty years. Then he removed him and set up David as their king, giving him his approval in these words: "I have found David son of Jesse to be a man after my own heart, who will carry out all my purposes." This is the man from whose posterity God, as he promised, has brought Israel a saviour, Jesus. John made ready for his coming by proclaiming baptism as a token of repentance to the whole people of Israel. And when John was nearing the end of his course, he said, "I am not what you think I am. No, after me comes one whose shoes I am not fit to unfasten."

" 'My brothers, you who come of the stock of Abraham, and others among you who revere our God, we are the people to whom the message of this salvation has been sent. . . .

" 'For these are our instructions from the Lord: "I have appointed you to be a light for the Gentiles, and a means of salvation to earth's farthest bounds" ' " (Acts 13:16-26, 47).

God's mighty acts among His people are at the heart of the Old Testament record. The whole Old Testament, in a sense, is based on the early proclamation of what God has done for Israel. In the early part of his synagogue sermon in Antioch of Pisidia recorded in Acts 13, Paul reviewed the movement of God's mighty acts in behalf of His people:

1. God chose the patriarchs.
2. God made the people great in Egypt.
3. God delivered them in the Exodus.
4. God undergirded them in the wilderness.
5. God destroyed the nations in Canaan and gave them their inheritance.
6. God raised up judges until Samuel the prophet.
7. God gave them Saul and later David as king.
8. God brought a Saviour from David's posterity.

Paul tied the story together. He showed how the God of the Old Testament and the God of the New Testament--of the old covenant and the new covenant--is the same God. God's redemptive activity moved toward a climax. The Old Testament references alluded to in I Peter 2:9, 10 (compare Isaiah 43:20, 21 and Hosea 1:9; 1:6; 2:23) highlight the fact that the Christian community became the new and true Israel. Because Christians--who were a non-people--have experienced divine mercy a significant responsibility rests on them: through blameless conduct they are to proclaim glorious deeds.

So Paul affirmed: We are the people to whom the message of this salvation has been sent and we are the means of salvation to earth's farthest bounds.

To Lead to Salvation

" 'Praise to the God of Israel:
For he has turned to his people, saved them and set them free,
and has raised up a deliverer of victorious power
    from the house of his servant David.
" 'So he promised: age after age he proclaimed
    by the lips of his holy prophets,
that he would deliver us from our enemies,
    out of the hands of all who hate us;
that he would deal mercifully with our fathers,
    calling to mind his solemn covenant.
" 'Such was the oath he swore to our father Abraham,
    to rescue us from enemy hands,
and grant us, free from fear, to worship him
    with a holy worship, with uprightness of heart,
    in his presence, our whole life long.
" 'And you, my child, you shall be called Prophet of the Highest,
for you will be the Lord's forerunner, to prepare his way
    and lead his people to salvation through knowledge of him,
    by the forgiveness of their sins:
for in the tender compassion of our God
    the morning sun from heaven will rise upon us,
to shine on those who live in darkness, under the cloud of death,
    and to guide our feet into the way of peace' "(Luke 1:68-79).

For centuries God is silent. Then one day His messenger appeared without warning to Zechariah. The angel explained to the priest that in his senior years he would father a son who would prepare the way for a new act of God. Until eight days after his son's birth, Zechariah was dumbfounded. Finally he broke out in jubilant praise as he gathered the echoes of the old covenant and fused them into a new outpouring of triumphant faith and hope--a psalm exalting God's glorious acts of salvation.

Zechariah called to mind the covenant. He may have recounted to himself the Old Testament reminders of God's working with His people--in trial and in joy, through failure and through accomplishment, by faithlessness and by faithfulness. Always there was God and His faithful witness reminding His people who they were and that through them God was seeking to bring all people to Him--working to fulfill His covenant.

This salvation would be a new exodus. The first Exodus from Egypt released God's people from their enemies so they could serve God in the way He commanded. So this new salvation would free Israel from Rome so they could worship with uprightness of heart.

"To shine on those who live in darkness." The original metaphor refers to a party of travelers overtaken by darkness before reaching their destination. They were terrified, expecting at any moment to be killed by beasts or enemies. All at once a bright light appeared to show them the way and they finished their trip in peace. These words point to the darkness among men before the Christ comes. But then the Saviour, the Light of the World, appears. Darkness is dispelled. Light illuminates the path to peace--reconciliation to God through Jesus the Christ.

To Announce Good News

"So he came to Nazareth, where he had been brought up, and went to synagogue on the Sabbath day as he regularly did. He stood up to read the lesson and was handed the scroll of the prophet Isaiah. He opened the scroll and found the passage which says,
'The spirit of the Lord is upon me because he has anointed me;
He has sent me to announce good news to the poor,
To proclaim release for prisoners and recovery of sight for the blind;
To let the broken victims go free,
To proclaim the year of the Lord's favour.'
He rolled up the scroll, gave it back to the attendant, and sat down; and all eyes in the synagogue were fixed on him.

"He began to speak: 'Today,' he said, 'in your very hearing this text has come true.' . . .

"Coming down to Capernaum, a town in Galilee, he taught the people on the Sabbath. . . .

"When day broke he went out and made his way to a lonely spot. But the people went in search of him, and when they came to where he was they pressed him not leave them. But he said, 'I must give the good news of the kingdom of God to the other towns also, for that is what I was sent to do' " (Luke 4:16-21, 31, 42, 43).

To begin His ministry Jesus returned to His hometown. The home folks were curious. Word had spread that Joseph's young Son was taking the country by storm. When He stood up in the synagogue--the sign used by a visiting rabbi to signal his desire to take charge of the service--the worshipers looked and listened. He read from Isaiah 61, gave the scroll back to the attendant, and sat down on a small platform intended for the speaker to deliver his message.

"All that the prophets have announced, all that Old Testament history has pointed toward, is today unrolling before your very eyes. These words which have just been read are at this moment coming to fulfillment--in me: I am the one anointed by God to proclaim the year of the Lord--the period which I am ushering in, in which God will grant salvation not only to Jews but to all who believe. I have come not merely to preach a solution, but to be the redeemer."

I must give the good news of the kingdom: Peter summarized what all of Christ's followers knew with certainty when he affirmed to the Jewish doctors of the law in Jerusalem, "There is no salvation in anyone else at all, for there is no other name under heaven granted to men, by which we may receive salvation" (Acts 4:12). The good news is that a new activity of God has broken forth in the world which confronts men with new possibilities as well as new demands. This salvation is a condition by which God will make life what it has not previously been--real living! Life full and abundant, significant and meaningful.

The central theme of the good news was the kingdom of God--the promise of eternal life. The kingdom came into the midst of men in the person and ministry of Jesus Christ as God's supreme gift to His people. It is both present and yet to come. In its essence Christianity is decisively oriented toward the future, in the direction of life which is eternal.

To Seek and to Save

"Entering Jericho he made his way through the city. There was a man there named Zacchaeus; he was superintendent of taxes and very rich. He was eager to see what Jesus looked like; but, being a little man, he could not see him for the crowd. So he ran on ahead and climbed a sycamore-tree in order to see him, for he was to pass that way. When Jesus came to the place, he looked up and said, 'Zacchaeus, be quick and come down; I must come and stay with you today.' He climbed down as fast as he could and welcomed him gladly. At this there was a general murmur of disapproval. 'He has gone in,' they said, 'to be the guest of a sinner.' But Zacchaeus stood there and said to the Lord, 'Here and now, sir, I give half my possessions to charity; and if I have cheated anyone, I am ready to repay him four times over.' Jesus said to him, 'Salvation has come to this house today!--for this man too is a son of Abraham, and the Son of Man has come to seek and save what is lost'" (Luke 19:1-10).

"Levi held a big reception in his house for Jesus; among the guests was a large party of tax-gatherers and others. The Pharisees and the lawyers of their sect complained to his disciples: 'Why do you eat and drink,'' they said, 'with tax-gatherers and sinners?' Jesus answered them: 'It is not the healthy that need a doctor, but the sick; I have not come to invite virtuous people, but to call sinners to repentance'" (Luke 5:29-32).

Salvation as Jesus preached it by His words and His deeds was for sinners. A man who is not sick, Jesus told His critics, doesn't need a doctor. Why He hobnobbed with the questionables was clear--they were the people who needed what He had to offer. Zacchaeus, the tax collector, is an example of a man who sensed that his life was empty, who got wind that Jesus could do something about it, and who pitted his whole existence on the radical ideas of his Dinner Guest.

In Luke 15 Jesus tells three stories which illustrate almost poetically how God seeks so that He might save. Like a shepherd who has lost one sheep and leaves 99 to look for it, so God searches after us in our lostness. Like a poor woman who sweeps and resweeps until she finds her lost coin, so God hunts for us in spite of how little we are. Like a forgiving father waiting anxiously to welcome a wayward son, so God stretches His arms of loving compassion, no matter how bad or wayward are His children.

Francis Thompson (1859-1907) intended to become a priest, then chose to study medicine. But being raised under the suffocating pressures of a hard father, he was unable to pass the examinations. He settled in London where he barely managed to keep alive, finally resorting to opium to deaden his misery. In his poverty he began to write poetry on scraps of paper and one day he slipped several under the door of a London journal. The editor spotted a true poet and hunted for the author. Finally finding Thompson, the editor was able to help him to God, who in turn reclaimed his life from despair. His masterpiece, "The Hound of Heaven," is a moving account of how God kept after him, never letting him go until finally He found him.

> *I fled Him, down the nights and down the days;*
> *I fled Him down the arches of the years;*
> *I fled Him down the labyrinthine ways*
> *Of my own mind. . . .*

Finally he halts long enough that Christ can speak to him:

> *Whom wilt thou find to love ignoble thee*
> *Save Me, save only Me?*

"Love ... and You Will Live"

"On one occasion a lawyer came forward to put this test question to him: 'Master, what must I do to inherit eternal life?' Jesus said, 'What is written in the Law? What is your reading of it?' He replied, 'Love the Lord your God with all your heart, with all your soul, with all your strength, and with all your mind; and your neighbour as yourself.' 'That is the right answer,' said Jesus; 'do that and you will live.'

"But he wanted to vindicate himself, so he said to Jesus, 'And who is my neighbour?' Jesus replied, 'A man was on his way from Jerusalem down to Jericho when he fell in with robbers, who stripped him, beat him, and went off leaving him half dead. It so happened that a priest was going down by the same road; but when he saw him, he went past on the other side. So too a Levite came to the place, and when he saw him went past on the other side. But a Samaritan who was making the journey came upon him, and when he saw him was moved to pity. He went up and bandaged his wounds, bathing them with oil and wine. Then he lifted him on to his own beast, brought him to an inn, and looked after him there. Next day he produced two silver pieces and gave them to the innkeeper, and said, "Look after him; and if you spend any more, I will repay you on my way back." Which of these three do you think was neighbour to the man who fell into the hands of the robbers?' He answered, 'The one who showed him kindness.' Jesus said, 'Go and do as he did' " (Luke 10:25-37).

The Samaritan's neighbor was not someone who lived next door to him back in Samaria. The neighbor was not found among the scores of needy in either Jerusalem (where he may have spent the night) or Jericho (his present destination). The Samaritan's neighbor was this poor fellow by the roadside. He had never seen him before. There were no natural claims to loyalty or devotion. The two were simply thrown together in the stream of history.

Who is the neighbor? He is this one *here* by the roadside, the ore in whose presence the Samaritan suddenly found himself as he came around a bend in the road. The neighbor is someone *here, now*; someone we have access to, someone we are close to, with whom we find ourselves.

Probably it is the failure to recognize this fact which is the main reason why Christians have so often been known to "pass by" on the other side. We are under the constant temptation to overlook the people lying at our feet in favor of those "anticipated neighbors" whom we hope to meet in Jericho, or those "past neighbors" who were left behind in Jerusalem or Samaria. But these are not the true neighbors. The one whom we are to love as ourselves is this needy one at our side, whoever he may be. He has a claim on all our resources, our time, and our compassion. This is a daring answer.

The New Testament is often accused of being idealistic in its commands. And to love your neighbor as yourself is certainly most idealistic when interpreted from this point of view. Yet Jesus offers the story of this Samaritan as the fulfillment of the command. And there is no hint that this incident is in any way unworthy of what it means to love your neighbor as you do yourself. Yet surely there is nothing idealistic about the Samaritan, and what he did. The story is utterly realistic and true to life. The Samaritan's example is challenging and difficult, to be sure. But there is not a one of us who, by God's grace, could not do as well as the Samaritan did.

"You Are the Witnesses"

"One day when he was praying alone in the presence of his disciples, he asked them, 'Who do the people say I am?' They answered, 'Some say John the Baptist, others Elijah, others that one of the old prophets has come back to life.' 'And you,' he said, 'who do you say I am?' Peter answered, 'God's Messiah.' Then he gave them strict orders not to tell this to anyone. And he said, 'The Son of Man has to undergo great sufferings, and to be rejected by the elders, chief priests, and doctors of the law, to be put to death and to be raised again on the third day.' . . .

"As they were talking about all this, there he was, standing among them. Startled and terrified, they thought they were seeing a ghost. But he said, 'Why are you so perturbed? Why do questionings arise in your minds? Look at my hands and feet. It is I myself. Touch me and see; no ghost has flesh and bones as you can see that I have.' . . .

"Then he opened their minds to understand the scriptures. 'This,' he said, 'is what is written: that the Messiah is to suffer death and to rise from the dead on the third day, and that in his name repentance bringing the forgiveness of sins is to be proclaimed to all nations. Begin from Jerusalem: it is you who are the witnesses to all this'" (Luke 9:18-22; 24:36-39, 45-48).

In P. W. Turner's *Christ in the Concrete City*, Mary tells the disciples, "After you went away I stayed beside the grave. I was crying because they wouldn't leave him alone even after they'd killed him. Then I turned away. And there was--a man-- standing there. I suppose I thought he was the gardener. And he asked me why I was crying. And I asked him to tell me where he had taken the body. I--I wanted to go and do what I could for him. And then he said 'Mary' (Yes, that's it--he said 'Mary' with the old inflection of voice) and I realized who he was. It was the Lord. It was the Lord, and I've seen him and he isn't dead anymore. He's alive."

And in that precise moment the reality of Easter confronted the human family. For it was Mary Magdalene who was used as God's messenger to first herald the good news about Jesus' conquest over death. She was the first to run forth to tell others the triumphant fact: I have seen the Lord.

In Mary's testimony we have the very essence of Christianity. As William Barclay has pointed out: "A Christian is essentially one who can say 'I have seen the Lord.' Christianity does not mean knowing about Jesus; it means knowing Jesus. It does not mean arguing about Jesus; it means meeting Jesus. It means the certainty of experience that Jesus is alive."

Mary personified the kind of witness Whittaker Chambers described when he wrote of himself, "I was a witness. I do not mean a witness against Alger Hiss and the others. A man is not primarily a witness *against* something. This is only incidental to the fact that he is a witness *for* something. A witness is a man whose life and faith are so completely one that when the challenge comes to step out and testify for his faith, he does so, disregarding all rules, accepting all consequences."

And this is exactly what many of the witnesses to the resurrection were called to do. Peter--crucified upside down. Paul--beheaded outside Rome. Stephen--stoned looking up to heaven. *You are the witnesses to all this.*

25

"Repent . . . and Receive"

"When they heard this they were cut to the heart, and said to Peter and the apostles, 'Friends, what are we to do?' 'Repent,' said Peter, 'repent and be baptized, every one of you, in the name of Jesus the Messiah for the forgiveness of your sins; and you will receive the gift of the Holy Spirit. For the promise is to you, and to your children, and to all who are far away, everyone whom the Lord our God may call.'

"In these and many other words he pressed his case and pleaded with them: 'Save yourselves,' he said, 'from this crooked age.' Then those who accepted his word were baptized, and some three thousand were added to their number that day.

"They met constantly to hear the apostles teach, and to share the common life, to break bread, and to pray. A sense of awe was everywhere, and many marvels and signs were brought about through the apostles. All whose faith had drawn them together held everything in common: they would sell their property and possessions and make a general distribution as the need of each required. With one mind they kept up their daily attendance at the temple, and, breaking bread in private houses, shared their meals with unaffected joy, as they praised God and enjoyed the favour of the whole people. And day by day the Lord added to their number those whom he was saving" (Acts 2:37-47).

Franz Kaafka, a perplexing 20th-century Czechoslovakian novelist, wrote a queer little story that he called "Metamorphosis." It is the tale of a man who awoke one morning to discover that during the night he had turned into a huge cockroach. The author gives a detailed account of the man's trials and tribulations as he lives his brief span as a cockroach, and then of his pathetic and tragic end.

He knows that he cannot turn himself back into a man and yet he will not accept that fact. There is nothing that he can do himself, yet he assures himself that there is. He fails repeatedly--but he tries again--to fail again. The story ends just where it started--the man is still a cockroach--except that on the last page he is a dead cockroach.

This is the story of our own lives. We resolve to change. We fail. We make a new vow. And a new failure. And new guilt for having failed. This circle of resolve and failure is broken only by death--except as it is broken by repentance.

To understand Christ--His salvation and His Gospel--demands more than the insight of our mind--to know who He was and what He did. It demands the allegiance of our whole being. Jesus Himself put it this way, "Repent, and believe in the Gospel" (Mark 1:15). Repentance and belief go together like bread and butter. To repent is to realize that you are at the end and then do something about it. Repentance means changing one's mind, turning about, going a new direction. To believe is to accept the good news that God |has acted in the Christ event and thus makes it possible for us to go in His direction.

Yet it is only as Christ is the content of our belief that we move into Christian faith. Having repented, we pause to receive the gift of the Holy Spirit. We must always remember that Christian faith is gift, not accomplishment. We can will to believe--but that is not faith. We can resolve to trust-- but that is not Christian faith. Only as God gives Himself to us in Christ and Christ becomes the object of our belief and the ground of our trust have we thought rightly about Jesus.

Life in Christ Jesus

"Let your conduct be worthy of the gospel of Christ, so that whether I come and see you for myself or hear about you from a distance, I may know that you are standing firm, one in spirit, one in mind, contending as one man for the gospel faith. . . .

"Let your bearing towards one another arise out of your life in Christ Jesus. For the divine nature was his from the first; yet he did not think to snatch at equality with God, but made himself nothing, assuming the nature of a slave. Bearing the human likeness, revealed in human shape, he humbled himself, and in obedience accepted even death--death on a cross. Therefore God raised him to the heights and bestowed on him the name above all names, that at the name of Jesus every knee should bow--in heaven, on earth, and in the depths-- and every tongue confess, 'Jesus Christ is Lord,' to the glory of God the Father.

"So you too, my friends, must be obedient, as always; even more, now that I am away, than when I was with you. You must work out your own salvation in fear and trembling; for it is God who works in you, inspiring both the will and the deed, for his own chosen purpose.

"Do all you have to do without complaint or wrangling. Show yourselves guileless and above reproach, faultless children of God in a warped and crooked generation, in which you shine like stars in a dark world and proffer the word of life" (Philippians 1:27; 2:5-15).

Menno Simons' life motto was penned on everything he wrote: "For other foundation can no man lay than that is laid, which is Jesus Christ" (I Corinthians 3:11). However, when we affirm that *Jesus is Lord* we take our stand not only with Menno but with first-century disciples as well. Paul emphasized over and over that salvation involves an initial declaration, boldly asserting that Jesus is Lord.

The earliest Christian affirmation or creed was simply "Jesus is Lord." To assert the creed carried with it the clear recognition that nothing else--Caesar, money, power, prestige, nothing--takes precedence. For the early Christians, the most dramatic use of this simple confession was in times of persecution. For the pagan Roman citizen, the apex of virtue was to confess that Caesar is Lord. Christians were demanded to renounce their faith and affirm, "Jesus be cursed." Yet many refused, and at the expense of their lives cried out, "Jesus is Lord."

To take our stand in the twentieth century along with our forebears means that in spite of the false gods which clamor for allegiance we too declare emphatically where our loyalty is lodged. C. S. Lewis put it this way in *Mere Christianity:* "I am trying here to prevent anyone saying the really foolish thing that people often say about Him: 'I'm ready to accept Jesus as a great moral teacher, but I don't accept His claim to be God.' This is the one thing we must not say. A man who was merely a man and said the sort of things which Jesus said would not be a great moral teacher. He would either be a lunatic--on a level with a man who says he is a poached egg--or else he would be the devil of hell. You must make your choice. Either this man was, and is, the Son of God: or else a madman or something worse. You can shut Him up for a fool, you can spit at Him and kill Him as a demon; or you can fall at His feet and call Him Lord and Lord."

Conduct worthy of the Gospel stems from boldly asserting where one's devotion is committed, followed by working out that salvation into all areas of life's complexities so that light continues to shine in a dark world.

God and His People Triumph

"After this I looked and saw a vast throng, which no one could count, from every nation, of all tribes, peoples, and languages, standing in front of the throne and before the Lamb. They were robed in white and had palms in their hands, and they shouted together:

" 'Victory to our God who sits on the throne, and to the Lamb!' And all the angels stood around the throne and the elders and the four living creatures, and they fell on their faces before the throne and worshipped God, crying:

" 'Amen! Praise and glory and wisdom, thanksgiving and honour, power and might, be to our God for ever and ever! Amen.' . . .

"Then I saw a new heaven and a new earth, for the first heaven and the first earth had vanished, and there was no longer any sea. I saw the holy city, new Jerusalem, coming down out of heaven from God, made ready like a bride adorned for her husband. I heard a loud voice proclaiming from the throne: 'Now at last God has his dwelling among men! He will dwell among them and they shall be his people, and God himself will be with them. He will wipe every tear from their eyes; there shall be an end to death, and to mourning and crying and pain; for the old order has passed away' " (Revelation 7:9-12; 21:1-4)!

"Although New Testament Christians doubtless prayed, as we do, 'Thy kingdom come. Thy will be done in earth, as it is in heaven,' and although they therefore doubtless worked and prayed for the improvement of the world in which they lived, their hope rested upon God, not merely upon what He could do in this world, but upon His high mysterious Purpose." So wrote J. B. Phillips in *New Testament Christianity*.

The Bible begins with creation. It ends with new creation. Between the beginning and end, however, the Scripture devotes considerable space to the hope of God's people. God's spokesman during Old Testament days looked forward to a new covenant, a new life, a new world. The New Testament reports how the kingdom dawned with the coming of Jesus Christ into the world and burst into noonday brightness as He established the new covenant. Eternal life is the new life which the Holy Spirit generates in that mysterious process which Jesus called "being born from above." The new birth issues in the new creation, as Paul explained, "When anyone is united to Christ, there is a new world; the old order has gone, and a new order has already begun" (II Corinthians 5:17).

As he wrote from Patmos, John commended some of the churches, rebuked others. To all he issued a call to repentance and a summons to steadfast loyalty to their Lord. Every man, John observed, will belong to either the beast or the Lamb. Finally, though, victory belongs to God and His people--they will triumph.

God's story begins with a man in a garden. It ends with a man in a city. But the city is a garden city with a river of the water of life flowing through its center and a tree of life planted in its midst. God here pictures both heaven and earth-- the eternal redeems the temporal. Like the Old Testament, so the New ends with a note of triumphant hope and eager expectation. God who has acted mightily in history, and supremely in Jesus Christ, will through Him perfect the new creation.

In the meantime we pray, "Our Father in heaven, thy name be hallowed; thy kingdom come, thy will be done, on earth as in heaven" (Matthew 6:9, 10).

31

FOR STUDY

1 / Facing a New Frontier

Akron, Ohio--January 3, 1965, marked the beginning of regular Sunday morning worship services for the Summit Christian Fellowship. Composed largely of professional persons, the group felt they needed opportunities for regular Bible study and fellowship--after meeting sporadically for two years. Although the group is somewhat mobile, with interns and social workers coming and going over a one- or two-year period, they have developed a sense of unity and identity that has molded them into an emerging congregation.

Champaign-Urbana, Illinois--Although Mennonites have resided here in small numbers for many years, they usually worshiped in adjacent communities. By 1962, sentiment favored establishing a permanent inter-Mennonite church to serve both residents and students. Member Leonard Neufeld said, "The major question we face is, 'What shall be the nature of our witness?' "

Bogota, Colombia--When missionary Howard Habegger saw me off at the Bogota airport he said enthusiastically, "Two people accepted the Lord yesterday." So reported mission board executive Andrew Shelly after a stop at Colombia's capital and a visit to the Mennonite congregation which organized just one week earlier. Only a few years ago Bogota's population was one million--now it is over 1,300,000.

Saskatoon, Saskatchewan--Nutana Park Mennonite Church is the proposed name for the new group that First Mennonite Church is planning to organize. A brotherhood meeting of the mother church voted to build a sanctuary for the new congregation with 375-seat capacity at a cost of $75,000. There are about 400 potential members in the Nutana area, on Saskatoon's east side.

Portland, Oregon--VS-er Leroy Chupp serves on the Community Concern Action Program, an interdenominational committee. In the immediate neighborhood of the Voluntary Service unit, 300 to 400 kids have few recreational facilities. Many are forced into the streets for lack of places to play. The community action group is trying, for one thing, to have certain streets closed to traffic part of the day to provide safe recreation areas. "We are convinced," Chupp says, "that if we are going to be effective in an interracial community, we will have to do more than come in and offer a little help and then hurry back to our own Mennonite ghettos."

Phoenix, Arizona--Where the Mennonite Church started a congregation 20 years ago in Phoenix, General Conference Mennonite for the most part joined other Protestant churches. However, in the late 1950s a Phoenix resident, Mrs. Ethel Rosenberger, tried to contact other area General Conference Mennonites through classified ads. This was the beginning of sensing the need for a General Conference congregation. In November, 1962, a house was purchased for a meeting place.

Hong Kong--To read that in 1841 this area was described as "a barren island with hardly a house upon it" seems incredible. Bulldozers are at work removing mountains and literally dumping them into the sea. As the city grows upward and outward in some sections, in other parts squatter huts perch like nests of cockroaches on the steep hillsides. The question confronting the Mennonite Church here is how to contribute Christian understanding most significantly. Two young men accepted Christ in the home of missionary James Stauffer on August 22 and are showing signs of growth. Possible locations for regular church services are being investigated.

Toronto, Ontario--The Mission Board Executive, the Finance Committee, and the City Committee and representatives of the Warden Park Church Council met to discuss strategy for the Warden Woods project. Consensus included--the church is already present in the Warden Woods community in the person of one or two families from Warden Park Church now living there; we must reach the family unit; ministering to people in their everyday problems is the best way to meet their needs; people are the church, therefore, we build the congregation first, then decide together the kind of facilities needed.

Dar es Salaam, Tanzania--With other countries of the world, Tanzania is experiencing an increasing tempo of trek to the cities. During an exploratory visit here in 1962, missionary Mahlon Hess had the names of 30 Mennonites then in the city. In 1965 the list increased to over 100 names. Pastor Daudi Mahemba, called to Dar es Salaam in 1964, has a vision of the opportunity and challenge posed by urban development.

Oklahoma City--Mennonite church workers of greater Oklahoma City, representing three conferences and five church projects, met October 25, 1965, for fellowship and discussion. Veterans in the group were D. J. and Linda Gerbrandt who began meeting with interested Mennonite families about eight years ago. They were the founders of the Western Oaks Mennonite Brethren Church in Bethany and are presently helping to form the Edmond Mennonite Brethren Church. Other congregations represented were the Mennonite Church Center, the City Rescue Mission, and Spencer Mennonite Church.

To most of us the word *frontier* brings images of covered wagons, log cabins, sturdy pioneers. Courage and vitality characterized the people of God in rugged frontier situations. Now our task is to consider the mission of today's church, living in increasingly urban situations, facing an equally demanding frontier. A certain romance surrounds stories of the Western frontier, but we are close enough to the modern city, have visited it often enough, that we feel no nostalgia or sentimentality about its knotty problems. We are often just far enough away to fear it, but not far enough that we can ignore it. For God's people today, the city is frontier--"a new field that offers scope for activity," or "the furthermost limits of achievement," to note the dictionary definition.

News excerpts which introduce this chapter were all clipped from church publications during 1964 and 1965. They illustrate varied facets of the contemporary frontier. Congregations are being established in urban areas not primarily because mission boards are sending professional evangelists. Rather, as the news briefs indicate, Mennonites are increasingly finding themselves living in urban situations. We must weigh the assertion made by Martin Marty in his booklet, *Babylon by Choice*: The new environment for the Christian mission is urban. Christians concerned with the future of their message will have to understand and, in a certain way, love the city.

Frontier Statistics

Most of us have seen a rural area transformed almost overnight into a housing development. The children's classic, *The Little House,* by Virginia Burton, is the story of a tiny house, built on a tree-dotted hillside, which is surrounded eventually by skyscrapers and elevated trains. The survival of the little house is a fanciful tale, but the account of the city gobbling

38

up the countryside is a true and realistic picture. A northern Indiana Mennonite, for example, lives in a small ranch home surrounded by two-story apartments, a large shopping center, a shoe store, and a filling station--all built within seven years.

Hundreds of cities growing like this add up to the statistic that two thirds of the United States population now live in metropolitan areas. In contrast, in 1900, 21 percent of the population was classified metropolitan. Between 1950 and 1960, according to the U.S. Census Bureau, the urbanized areas increased from 13,000 square miles to 25,000 square miles.

The picture in Canada is similar--in 1961 seven out of ten Canadians lived in urban centers with a population in excess of 1,000, as compared with four in ten in 1900. Of seventeen metropolitan areas, all but three had an increase of at least 30 percent between 1951 and 1961. Calgary and Edmonton almost doubled in size. Montreal grew by 43 percent, Toronto by 51 percent.

Statistics on urban growth in other areas of the world are even more astronomical. In Africa, for example, the number of people living in cities of 100,000 population increased over the first 50 years of this century by 629 percent. In 1900 there were ten cities in the world with a population of a million; today there are 120 such cities. The only statistics more astounding than those telling of urban growth in the past 50 years are those which chart predicted urban growth.

Statistics Mean People

But statistics are meaningful only as they are realized in terms of human situations and needs. Shakespeare asked, "What is the city but the people?" Where have the people come from? Where are they going?

Our first quick answer to, "Where have they come from?" tells part of the story--from the farm. When a sociologist informed 94-year-old John Eli Miller that he had a record number of 410 living descendants, he replied, "Where will they all find farms?" In Canada, 40 percent of the labor force was employed in agriculture in 1900, but only 10 percent in 1962.

Studies in the General Conference Mennonite Church in the United States indicated that in 1960, about one third of the employed members were still farmers, in comparison to only 4 percent for the nation. However, it is important to note that in both instances the proportion of farmers is rapidly on the decline--among General Conference Mennonites, the percentage of farmers dropped from 54 percent in 1943 to 31 percent in 1960, while in the general population the percentage dropped from 10 to 4 percent.

A Mennonite sociologist wrote in 1946, "Certainly no environment is more favorable for the perpetuation of the non-resistant faith than is the rural community; and for this reason the Mennonite churches will do well to keep themselves established in such communities, with a high percentage of their members directly engaged in agriculture." [1] In the intervening twenty years, however, the handwriting on the wall--or at least the scribbling on the granary door--has become increasingly clear. Without much choice, and perhaps without realizing it, Mennonites are part of a culture which has rapidly become urban.

During the decade from 1950 to 1960, when urban population figures were zooming upward, one rural county in Iowa showed a population loss of 8 percent. During that time, there was also a decrease in the number of farms in the county. It added up, for this county, to fewer, bigger farms--and ex-farmers looking elsewhere for work. An occupational survey of five Mennonite congregations in Iowa showed that in 1957, 43 percent of the employed persons were farmers; in 1965 this figure was down to 29 percent.

A Clan Dispersed

The experience of a particular family is typical--call them the Yoders. Father Yoder was the oldest of ten children, and all his brothers and sisters were now settled on farms in the surrounding area; ten miles was the longest distance he needed to drive to visit any one of them. Similarly, Mother Yoder's brother and sisters lived on farms within five miles. When Jim, the oldest of the five Yoder children, went to a church college in 1951, two teenage brothers remained at home to help with the work on the 120-acre farm.

After Jim went off to college, his aunts and uncles on both sides of the family tried to schedule the "get-together" times when he was home for vacation. But this became more difficult each year--one cousin left for VS several hundred miles away, another went to a different college, Jim's next younger brother volunteered for I-W. It was impossible to have all the cousins together, even at Christmas.

Today, fifteen years after Jim (one of the oldest of the first cousins) went away to college, five of his uncles are working part or full time at jobs other than farming (two have moved to a town twenty miles away); five of Jim's aunts are working part time in towns five to forty miles away; Jim's cousins are scattered from Idaho to Pennsylvania--plus one foreign country! Of the 30 first cousins in the clan who are out of high school, only six still live on a farm.

In the space of one generation--fifteen years--this clan has become dispersed and in many ways, urban. Although most of Jim's aunts and uncles have not actually moved to town, improved highways and more and faster cars have brought them closer to many cities.

The Frontier Is Where the Jobs Are

Menno Simons, speaking of the need for ministers to support themselves, admonished in 1544, "Rent a farm, milk cows, learn a trade if possible, do manual labor as did Paul." Today science and industrial technology have so altered our world that the job choices have drastically changed. The forces which have enabled fewer farmers to produce more food are the same ones which have been basic factors in the mushrooming of cities.

As the industrial revolution of the eighteenth century gave the first great push to the growth of cities, so the scientific and technological revolution of the century pushes people into many different occupational possibilities. Think about the people in your community who are working at jobs which did not even exist 20 or 30 years ago. In one urban Ohio congregation, for example, this list would include some of the factory machinists, the engineers, the neurology resident, the supervisor in the electronics factory.

Families and individuals, however, do not think in terms of scientific advances and statistics. For them, the move from a Virginia farm into Washington, D.C., or from a village in Maine to New York City, may be merely an attempt to realize the great American dream of getting ahead. Developments in transportation and communication, which have made the cities possible, have also created desire and possibility to be on the move.

A Worldwide Phenomenon

In considering the growth of urban areas, the fact that there are vastly more people in the world now than there ever were before cannot be overlooked. Between now and the year 2000, our population is expected to double--we can hardly imagine what this will mean. We can look at it another way: Because of the combination of population explosion and urbanization, the world will need in the next forty years as many new homes as have been built in the history of civilization up to this time. [2]

These forces are at work around the world, in varying degrees and speeds. For example, India, a village-organized nation with 600,000 small villages, is changing fast. One observer describes the situation this way: Dams are being built, radio-television centers are coming into being, airports are common. India's long-overpopulated cities are growing at a dizzying pace. Technology has come upon the scene. This means that people do not live where they work. It means that they no longer produce all the needs of their own life. Instead they will be employed to produce part of a product that will be sold in a remote place and attached to another product to be used by someone never seen before. The worker ceases planting. He enters a world where barter falls from prominence. He is part of a money world and he must be employed in order to have money.

India's greatest problem in relation to its meager food supplies is unemployment. From 50 to 100 million people are currently without jobs. The most recent Five-Year Plan, a plan that utilizes every bit of India's developmental forces, dreams of providing jobs for 10 million of these unemployed. There is one difficulty in this picture. By the end of the plan, even if 10 million jobs can have been provided, India's population will have grown by 15 million.[3]

The New Frontier Is You

We have looked at some of the forces producing urbanization--the directions of science and technology, especially as it affects agriculture; the population explosion; greater mobility, whether for young people seeking education or for families desiring greater economic security; rapid transportation and communication. In this study we want to understand more clearly the process of urbanization and to face squarely the implications which confront the people of God.

The place to begin is where you are. This is not a mission study of workers out there, or over yonder, or down under. William Stringfellow, a Christian attorney in East Harlem, says that a frontier is wherever the Gospel is brought to bear by the church on the life of the world.

For Discussion

1. Geographically, what is your church community? If you map in the areas touched by members' homes and job locations, how large would the circle be?

2. What industry has come into your community in the past five years?

3. What new persons have moved into the community, and where have they moved from?

4. How have shopping habits changed in the past five years?

5. How has your congregation changed in the past ten years-- occupationally, in level of education, in income level? Where are your nonresident members?

---

1. Hershberger, Guy F., *War, Peace and Nonresistance* (Scottdale: Herald Press, 1944), p. 29.
2. Shinn, Roger L., *Tangled World* (New York: Scribner's, 1965), p. 64.
3. Marty, Martin, *Babylon by Choice* (New York: Friendship Press, 1965), p. 30.

2 / Meeting City Expansion

Twenty years ago, five acres of low value swamp land were purchased for a few thousand dollars. Today the same five acres adjoin a gigantic shopping center and are worth nearly $200,000 to a large motel chain. This then-and-now story of the real estate situation of the Friendship Church near Cleveland, Ohio, is a dramatic example of the city enveloping the countryside. One of the persons who was part of the initial vision and growth of this congregation was Dale Nofziger. He told the story this way:

"The community has changed drastically. Naturally the church has reflected this change. The original area where we began having Sunday school has been cleared out by the freeway. Many of these people relocated in the same general area-- particularly those who had identified with the church. The original community of the early 1950's was people who had moved out of Cleveland during the early years of World War II when housing in the city was in short supply. They built their own homes on a do-it-yourself basis. Some were shacks, as there were no building codes in force, others were nicer. The later development of the whole postwar housing program swallowed up many of the shacks and a typical suburban culture was born.

"The people are basically the same, but they reflect the higher income level of the 60s. This is a factor hardly understood unless experienced and remembered--that people are better off today than they were in 1953, yet their cultural concepts are hidden by the low-down-payment home, beautifully landscaped with borrowed money."

Originally meeting in a home, the church group was informal and spontaneous. If a pressing need arose, a member might call an impromptu prayer meeting at any hour. The Sunday morning congregation included some families who drove in from established congregations, but was primarily local people. Later a modest cement block church house was erected. The name of the church, Friendship, indicated something of the purpose of the group.

Today the congregation has grown to a membership of just over a hundred. It is a block away from one of the largest shopping centers in North America; it is surrounded by freeways, and city planners call for more expressways. Most immediately, the church is surrounded by ever-higher apartment houses. The Friendship congregation is facing up to the tough questions of how to be God's people in this complex situation.

How can their acres of high-value land be used for the good of the community and for more effective Christian witness? Many of the members are homeowners, and find it hard to visualize the church's ministry to the local apartment house population. (Regardless of income, apartment house dwellers are assumed by the home-owning part of the population of a city to be somewhat irresponsible; they certainly are more mobile.)

The whole question of a church name, and what it communicates, was a recent question faced by the congregation. They must also consider what the architecture of their building says to the new community. The building which seemed adequate formerly, now looks dwarfed and insignificant between the apartment buildings. As Friendship wrestles with concerns such as these, they know their community is changing so rapidly that by the time answers emerge, the questions are different.

*I*n chapter 1 we looked at the movement from the country to the city, and the forces pressing that direction. Now we look at the other side of the coin, the gobbling up of the country by the city. As one writer has expressed it, cities are being turned inside out! City dwellers attempting to escape to more rural areas find that shopping centers and businesses rapidly follow them. How is the city growing? And where is it growing?

City Gobbles Country

The United States census bureau in 1960 lists 215 Standard Metropolitan Statistical Areas--a central city of 50,000 or more, with connected areas of dense population around it. Our word *metropolis* is from Greek words meaning mother city. As cities spilled into each other, a new word was needed to describe the super-metropolis--*megalopolis* is that word. It combines the Greek *megal*, meaning large or of giant size, with the *polis*, or city concept.

Megalopolis bursts the old boundaries, spanning states, cultures, and climates. The Atlantic seaboard, from Boston to Washington, D.C., has been cited as one example of megalopolis. Other examples would be the urban complex growing around the Great Lakes--with the Buffalo-Akron-Cleveland communities merging into the Chicago-Milwaukee complex. The geographic size and complexity of present-day New York City will be found in perhaps half a dozen other places in North America by the end of the century.

Megalopolis is difficult to define and describe because it is formless. The growth and expansion of cities takes place in many directions at once, and without any overall plan. Static definitions which described urban centers of other ages no longer fit. Like the western frontier of North American history, which changed with every wagon trek, so today's cities must be described in terms of movement. Recognizing the risk of over-

47

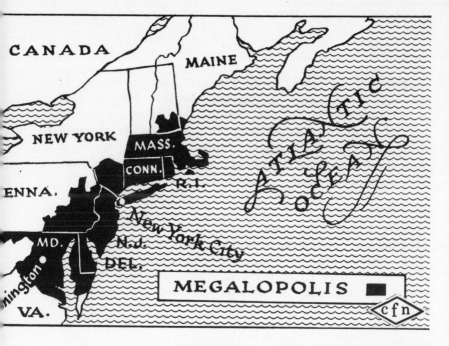

*MEGALOPOLIS--the jaw-breaking term coined to describe
the merging of metropolitan areas. One of these--the string
of cities and towns reaching from Boston to the District of
Columbia and beyond--is the wealthiest, most industrialized
area on earth. It includes 32 metropolitan areas stretching
through 10 states and holds 40 million people--more than live
in all of Mexico.*

simplifying a complicated process, we should note some general
areas of city life and growth.

Push from the Center

Inner city, now a common word in mission reports and
church publications, refers to the central business core of a city
and the immediately surrounding area of deterioration and low-
income housing. Although shopping centers and suburban business

districts are providing vigorous competition, the central core of our largest cities still holds the heart of banking and merchandising; it remains the nerve center for highly specialized persons and services which coordinate many aspects of life in the whole metropolitan area.

Years ago, this city core was typically surrounded by a ring of stately, dignified homes. As transportation improved and the original handsome buildings began to show their age, families who could afford to, moved "out." In many cases, real estate speculators bought vacated properties, and a vicious circle of exploitation began. The land itself might be valuable if it was needed for commercial purposes. In the meantime, landlords charged the highest possible rent while spending the absolute minimum for upkeep. Many of the results we today call slums.

The inner city is the home of the cities' newcomers. For almost a century prior to World War I, foreign-born immigrants replenished the labor force of our cities. Their story was familiar-- arriving with few possessions, little ability in the English language, they settled in clusters wherever the rent was cheapest. Most of them, by working hard, were able eventually to move to better surroundings. In a generation or two many were absorbed into the mainstream of American life, with few of the distinguishing national characteristics left.

Recent Migrations into the City

Not everyone, however, was able to move out of the transition neighborhoods. Most recently, the migration into the cities has been primarily rural whites, Negroes, and Puerto Ricans. For the Negroes especially, the blighted areas have become traps. Limited job opportunities, poor schools, and segregated housing and a climate of defeat and inferiority have kept them from the social and economic mobility which foreign-born immigrants have experienced.

An important factor for the church to consider is that many of the newer groups moving into the heart of the city are not predominantly Roman Catholic in background, as were immigrants of earlier years. On the near north side of Chicago's

Loop, for example, thousands of southern whites have clustered in one strip of rundown apartments. Families in the South hear from northern relatives of job opportunities. They load up the old jalopy, head north, and move in with the relatives. Unskilled, they are the last hired and first fired. Bare feet, summer clothing, fear of noisy, complex transportation systems, unfamiliarity with such basics as the garbage can--all these speak of unpreparedness for the abrupt transition from rural to urban life. The church makes little impact because traditional Protestantism seems to them cool and impersonal. As one migrant to Chicago said, "Back home the churches were more noisy, friendly, and fun."

The inner city is often described in terms of the concentration of delinquency and crime. While inner city residents are more frequently involved with police and courts than are suburban dwellers, they are also the most powerless and voiceless in coping with police and the courts.

People More Important Than Place

The inner city may be found at places other than the geographic center. It may be across the tracks, or by the mill. The place does not matter, but the people do. They are, by and large, the newcomers, the residue of the older immigrant groups, those who have come to the city with dreams of improving their lot--only to discover hardships of a new and even more baffling kind.

One Mennonite city pastor described the inner city this way: "Multitudes come from everywhere for job privileges and better opportunities. In the city, wealth and poverty exist side by side; cultural beauty of the arts is within driving minutes of squalor, crime, robbery, rape, theft, and loneliness.

"Ghettos are another characteristic--human traps which go 15 stories or higher in the air; centers of poverty, poor education, school dropouts, unemployment, large families, public assistance, and broken homes. One of these buildings, housing 150 families with children, has less than 20 bona fide husbands. Inner city people are on the move. A parade of 1,500 people move in and out of Chicago every day. Instability results from this influx.

50

The churches are poor and cannot support a full-time pastor. A great spiritual vacuum exists." [1]

Communities in Transition

Those families who make it in the central city--father secures a steady job, mother works, children adjust to city schools-- move as quickly as possible to more desirable surroundings. Large areas of one-family-house neighborhoods are the next step between the tenement and the ranch-house-suburb. Typically, a house in such a community might become vacant, and be sold to a young family from a crowded tenement further downtown. If this family is of a different cultural background, another family of similar background moves in soon. At this point unscrupulous real estate men often attempt to create panic among the older residents of the community, urging them to sell their homes quickly and move out before the value of their property goes down. In a matter of months the whole character of the neighborhood may change.

Where, in this kind of transition, are God's people? The Danforth Mennonite Church in Toronto illustrates a congregation facing a rapidly changing community. The Protestant churches of the area are hardly touching the influx of persons of Greek and Italian descent, many of whom do not speak English. To further complicate the scene, a new subway line is to be built just behind the church, and the immediate area has been rezoned for apartment buildings. A chain store wants the church property. Determining God's strategy in this situation is a demanding task facing this sixty-year-old congregation.

The Flight to the Suburbs

Moving out from the heart of the city, one finds progressively more expensive homes, more costly educational facilities, higher incomes. There are of course exceptions, such as the "gold coast" apartments of some cities, which stand alongside slum areas. More commonly, however, the climb up the economic ladder is synonymous with the flight out from the central city.

Suburban areas, as within the city limits, include infinite

varieties of communities. There are the familiar developments of row houses, with block after block of small, inexpensive homes, each with a dot of lawn, TV, and a car. In another community, homes must cost $50,000 and up. Although considerable contrast exists between suburban communities, conformity within a given neighborhood is the rule--it is a suburb of workers or a suburb of bosses, and a change in the status of a man's job often assumes a change in his place of residence. A folk song currently popular describes the conformity of life in suburbia:

> Little boxes on the hillside,
> Little boxes made of ticky-tacky,
> Little boxes on the hillside,
> Little boxes all the same.
> There's a green one and a pink one
> And a blue one and a yellow one,
> And they're all made out of ticky-tacky
> And they all look just the same.

Suburbia has been described as "a way of life and a state of mind." Someone else defined a suburbanite as one who works in the city, lives where there is more space, and can afford to commute between the two. More specifically, *suburban* is defined as any census tract in a metropolitan area in which 2/3 of the families own their own homes and in which both income and number of children are above the national average. Although most families consider suburban life an escape from the city, this distinction is largely a myth. In reality, the suburbs are another part of the city.

Growth in Suburbs Accelerated

Several factors combine to account for the phenomenal growth of suburban areas in recent years. Easy transportation makes it possible for men to seek the advantages of both city and country life. Mortgage credit encourages families to own a home--or at least pay on one owned by the mortgage holder!

More recently, as new expressways have accelerated the movement of industries to outlying regions, a new phenomenon of out-commuting has grown. Now the traffic of blue-collar workers

52

traveling outward flows against the incoming traffic. The automobile, which has helped make suburban life possible, is choking it.

Many suburbs have grown up around little country towns. Thus many churches once located in a small town, serving a rural community, have been surrounded by families whose economic life centers in the city. In other instances, whole new communities have grown up in outlying areas.

Communities have sprung up around particular industries, as employment opportunities suddenly opened for hundreds of unskilled workers. These communities are dependent upon a particular industry for their livelihood, and during strikes or underemployment, results are felt drastically. They often have fewer community resources than those suburbs which have developed more slowly, and thus a higher incidence of crime and delinquency.

Church in Suburbia

The rapidly growing suburbs have been the scene of rapidly growing Protestant churches. Looking at buildings and programs, the picture would appear bright. But the fact that one author titles a book *The Suburban Captivity of the Churches* indicates that there is a darker side to the picture. "As the Negroes have come into the inner city," a Mennonite pastor has observed, "the Protestants have fled. The educated people live in the suburbs. They commute to pluck the fruits downtown and rush back in the evening to water their lilies. The farther out one lives, the higher his office in Chicago's Loop." [2]

Many dark pictures are painted--the church has run away from the inner city; it is operating as a cozy social club in the suburbs. Because the Mennonite Church has been primarily rural in this country, we are not exempt from concern. The story of Friendship Church in Cleveland pinpoints the fact that for many congregations, whether they like it or not--the die is cast--the city has encompassed them. Their problem is how to be God's people in this changed environment. The story of another Mennonite community which has become part of suburbia was in a recent *Christian Living* article of which excerpts follow.

53

*T*hirty minutes by car from Niagara Falls, lies Alden, New York. Situated just east of the city of Buffalo, Alden is the heart of a rather young Mennonite community which has almost completely changed since its beginning.

When Mennonites first came to Alden in 1923-30, they were mostly farm families. But with a large city nearby these people soon felt the pressures of what one might call "creeping urbanization." Today in the Alden Mennonite Church, for example, only four of the 175 members are full-time farmers. Within just one generation this church has changed almost entirely from a rural to an urban setting.

During the early twenties industrial developments in Buffalo were drawing many of the area's farm workers into the higher-paying jobs. Farm labor became expensive, and older people were forced to sell their farms. Here was good land at a relatively cheap price for the Mennonite families of other areas looking for economic opportunities. The city of Buffalo provided an excellent market for milk, vegetables, and produce. And for the few nonfarmers or the part-time farmers there were employment possibilities in the nearby city.

With all these opportunities for the farms of the area why did the Mennonites begin leaving the land so soon after they had arrived in the area? I see the main reason in the lack of economic advancement in farming. As the city of Buffalo expanded, new jobs opened for construction workers and salesmen. And with the city approaching, land prices began to rise as did the price of machinery.

Take John Bontrager, Jr., for example. After working as a tenant farmer for a short time, John began to hire himself out to a construction company in Buffalo. With some experience he decided to take on subcontract work and hire his own men. In 1949 he built his own lumber and supply yard, hiring carpenters, yardmen, and secretaries. Today Bontrager constructors build an average of 60 to 70 houses a year in eight different housing projects east of Buffalo.

By the 1940's carpentry was the number-one vocation among the members of the Alden Mennonite Church. Young people considered carpentry as the vocation with most opportunities for creative work with increased pay. Older farmers sold their farms because none of their children were interested in continuing with that work.

Farming is still the occupation for four members of the Alden Church. It is interesting to note, however, that all of these live east of Alden, approximately 20 to 30 miles away from the urban area of Buffalo. Here land prices are moderate and taxes lower.[3]

The article goes on to discuss the effect of urbanization on the life of the Mennonite community--which is the subject of chapter 3.

For Discussion

1. If yours is a rural congregation, what interchange have you had in the past year with any churches in the nearest large city?

2. Consider a large city near your community:
   a. How do you benefit because of this city?
   b. What is a major problem this city is facing?
   c. Does your congregation have any responsibility toward the people of this city?

3. "I want to live in a suburb of all white, all middle-class families while my children are young; they should not have to cope with the problems of the world yet." How do you feel about this statement?

---

1. Horst, Laurence, in an address at the June, 1965, annual meeting of the Mennonite Board of Missions (Goshen, Ind.).
2. *Ibid.*
3. Bontrager, Edwin, "The Farmer, The Carpenter, The Cabinetmaker" in *Christian Living*, July, 1965.

3 / Encountering Urbanization

To continue the story begun in chapter 2, the Mennonite community in western New York has undergone many changes. This is evident not only in the occupational and economic life but also in a different pattern of relationships between the brotherhood and a changed social status in the community.

The most obvious change has come in the financial status of the Mennonite families. In the twenties and during the depression the standard of living was low and the economy simple. Today most of the families enjoy a more-comfortable-than-average way of life.

Has the improved economic position of its members meant a disintegration of brotherhood relationships within the church? Bishop David Beachy thinks not. He says that the spirit of fellowship exists as much today, although perhaps in a different quality than in the days when farmers lived close together and shared their work.

David also feels that the faster way of life in the urban environment has not broken down relationships between people. Instead he says, "In fact, I have more opportunities to learn to know people today than I used to." There still seems to be healthy interaction at both the church's formal and informal gatherings.

"How has this vocational change affected the young people

of this area in the last decade and a half?" Author Edwin Bontrager asked David.

"Well, I believe it has led young people today to take more of an active interest in the church than they did when I was young," he replied. David cited interest in MYF as an example.

Much of this increased interest in the church and its activities can be attributed to church schools. For many years few people left the Mennonite community for more than a six-week winter Bible school session. In the past eight years, however, 36 young people from Alden have gone to church high schools, 23 to college, and one to seminary.

Another interesting aspect of the trend from rural to urban in the Mennonite life of Alden has been their effect on the surrounding community. Whereas in the past the Mennonites were known as good farmers or hard workers, today many would characterize them by honest living and aggressiveness in many different occupations. Many no longer see the Mennonites as a separatist group but rather as a people with a clearcut witness as they reach out beyond themselves.

The main reason for this latter reaction is the fact that the community is coming into contact with Mennonites as individuals who witness for Christ through their work and their leisure time. They have met and worked with Joe Miller, interior decorator for Bontrager Construction Company, or heard the voice of Gerald Jantzi announcing on Buffalo's WDCX-FM. Or they may have bought a book in Richard Bender's store or become acquainted with Joseph Erb as one of the administrators of the downtown city mission. Some of their children may be in Joseph Baer's classes in the public high school, or their house may have been built by contractor Allen Erb.

This interaction with the community is perhaps the best result of the country-to-city trend in this area. Today the Mennonites of Alden know that the rest of the community exists about them, and they are living, working, and praying for its benefit. Thus the rural to urban move, while it has meant the loss of some ideals and traditions, has also been the gain of responsibilities and opportunities even more valuable. [1]

*H*aving noted the growth of cities, and some of the forces producing that growth, we have observed urban life in terms of quantities--sizes of cities, kinds of growth, directions of growth. Now it is time to look squarely at the larger implications of this process called urbanization. We are talking about the style and manner of our life today, whether we live on the farm, or in a suburban ranch house, or in a high-rise apartment complex.

In *The Changing Church in Canada,* Stewart Crysdale has summarized urbanism helpfully. He pointed out that urbanism is more than residence in an urban center--it is an ethos or style of life, now for the first time shared by a majority of Canadians and Americans from coast to coast.

As a style of life, urbanism means being open to new ideas, always ready to question old norms. It means the growth of rationality in everyday life. People do things not so much because they want to, but because such routines produce desired results--a regular paycheck, for instance. Urbanism implies living in close touch with people whose religion, color, language, and customs may be different from our own. No longer is the community dominated by white, Anglo-Saxon, Protestants.

Urbanism involves rapid interchange of ideas, through personal contact or through mass media--television, radio, newspapers, books, and magazines. An urbanized person moves in several circles and belongs to a wide variety of organizations--social, occupational, cultural, religious. He has access to a dazzling array of commodities and services.

Such a complex pattern of living depends upon and in turn produces a high degree of specialization in work. It frequently is accompanied by bigness, objectivity, efficiency and standardization in different kinds of organizations. Urbanized people tend to be mobile. One in four families moves each year in Canada. They change jobs more frequently than neighbors whose urbanism is lower. [2]

Part of an Affluent Society

As Christians in the late twentieth century, one facet of urbanization we need to face is the affluence of our society. In the affluent society, more people own, use, or consume more things than men ever have possessed or thought possible. In the United States and Canada, doctors more often warn people about eating too much than too little. Agricultural surpluses pose a greater problem than shortages. Most people have the clothing they need, if not all they want. Americans own about 36 motor vehicles for every 100 persons; cars occupy 23 times as many square feet of land in America as do people! They average several radios per family, and a television set for nearly every three persons. Americans are producing more and more things with fewer man-hours of work.

Most people in the affluent society do not consider themselves rich. A majority are straining hard to get along. Many people want a lot; they want at least a little more than the people around them. And nobody has figured out how most people can have more than the people around them.

To live and function in the affluent society without multiplying possessions is almost impossible. The illustrations of the fact are everywhere. For most of the world's three billion people an automobile is an almost incredible luxury. In our affluent society many people cannot earn a living without a car. As for housing, past generations and many families in our cities today would consider central heating, elaborate plumbing, electric lights and refrigeration, and elevators to be impressive luxuries. In the affluent society a city would die in its filth and confusion if it lost these. The former luxuries have become basic necessities for masses of people. [3]

One of the criticisms frequently leveled at the suburban church--and this could include nearly any congregation outside the central city--is that it suffers a disabling kind of near-sightedness. Living in unprecedented comfort, members are unable to respond to the urgent needs and problems which the majority of the world's population suffers.

As one writer said, "Two beautiful worlds are growing up

in the suburbs. One is the world of the gadget--the lovely world of color TV, deepfreezes, big hi-fis, two cars in the garage and tranquilizing drugs in the medicine cabinet. This world is not of itself bad. The other world is the world of the presumably spiritual: the world of the crowded churches, long lines at the communion rail, small group meetings, good will, and noble intentions. This world is not of itself enough. The basic trouble is that few suburbanites see any connection between the world of the gadget and the world of the spirit. The intimate relationship between the Lord's Supper and the new migrant in the heart of the city is not evident to them. They are not aware of the connection between their own abundance and starvation in India or poverty of their own central city. It is to this basic secularism of suburbia that the suburbanite prophet must address himself."

Increasingly Interdependent and Impersonal

In a report of a mountain congregation in Virginia, the author said, "A high percentage of the members have factory jobs in the nearby town of Waynesboro, where acquaintances are made and friendships shared."

All of us have become increasingly dependent on the services of people we do not know. Clerks, cashiers, repairmen, telephone operators--our lives touch a complicated web of services and agencies at many points. As this happens, we are not so concerned with the character of the people involved, but the quality and efficiency of their service to us. We may not know whether the meter reader is married or single, joyful or burdened with cares--he simply comes and goes once a month.

One writer in the Encyclopedia of the Social Sciences touched on the interdependence of city life when he defined urbanism as "the movement of people from communities concerned chiefly or solely with agriculture to other communities, generally larger, whose activities are primarily centered in government, trade, manufacture or allied interests."

Part of the Transportation/Communication Revolution

A resident of Chicago, attending a conference-wide church

meeting about 60 miles from his home, was chatting with the local young people. When he invited the youth to visit him in Chicago sometime, he was startled by their casual assurance that "We just might do that. We run in to Chicago Sunday night after church sometimes!" He had not realized before how close to his doorstep "the country" had come!

But even without traveling to the city, our lives and values are increasingly influenced by communications from the city. How many women read at least one monthly women's magazine where everything from hair-dos to recipes is geared for the sophisticated, highly urbanized white woman? When planning a new house, we look to the *American Home* and *Better Homes and Gardens* for our ideas. These illustrations are pointed out not as being wrong, but simply as indications of our involvement with the values and pressures of middle-class American life.

Robert Spike, in *Safe in Bondage,* put it this way. "The city is very much in the country. There are television antennas on nearly every permastone-covered house. The young people are graduated from modernistic brick high schools, where they have been instructed in world history and from which they have taken trips with the marching band to all the metropolitan centers within the range of the school bus."

Part of increasing urbanization is the increase of information any person receives--whether the ideas and contacts come by way of casual meetings with many people, the multitude of magazines and books readily available, or by TV and radio. We are constantly bombarded with impressions and ideas, and do not have time to digest them and to weigh them against our values and convictions.

Question the Old Tradition

With so many influences bombarding the individual, the traditions and assumptions he has learned from his parents come into question. At the same time that mass production and mass advertising media are in many ways pushing us toward conformity to middle-class standards, we are finding ourselves part of an age that questions traditional values and standards.

Mennonite minister John E. Lapp has noted the questioning of certain values related to homelife. "In the past the family was guided by customs received from its forefathers. Changes in homelife were slow to come, and life usually continued as it had been practiced by ancestors with minor changes from generations to generation. But now in this computer age many changes come to us in one generation.

"The greatest factor bringing these changes into the life of the family is the fact that we no longer live in the 'closed Mennonite community.' Barriers of language and culture, rural agricultural life, and even the distinctive dress of separated Christians no longer exist. Our families now live in well-populated neighborhoods and use modern conveniences of all types. As a result our Christian way of life comes under the scrutiny and questioning of non-Christian neighbors. Education no longer ends at the elementary or secondary level, but thousands of youth attend college and graduate school each year. All of these factors combine to bring change into the home and family life of our Mennonite communities." [4]

A Typical Situation

In 1964, a detailed church planning study of Medina County, Ohio, was made by the Regional Church Planning Office in Cleveland. The situation and the implications for the church are typical enough to include here some excerpts of the 94-page report.

For more than a century Medina County was an agricultural county with a total population of less than 25,000 persons. During the 1940s this picture began to change--agriculture on the decline, population rising and changing in composition (for example one-half of all workers are now commuters). This 424-square-mile county still appears to be largely rural as one flies over it or drives through it. However, this is very deceptive since today about one-half of the residents live in urban surroundings and another 40 percent live in an environment which is urban in every respect except the census definition of the word. Urbanization is evident in water supply problems, growth of recreational facilities (golf courses), and in the demand for public services.

The county is entering an era which will be marked by vast changes. However, many of the residents are opposed to change in general and strongly opposed to the rapid changes which accompany the urbanization of a rural county. The resulting tensions will have a major impact on the decision-making process both inside and outside the local church.

Speaking of specific congregations in the area, the report says of one Mennonite church, "The congregation has an outstanding stewardship record, a spectacular location, a fine building, a great sense of loyalty--but it needs to develop a statement of purpose and a set of goals which are consistent with its reason for being at this location at this point in history. Only a few of the members are still full-time farmers but the congregation does not appear to have adjusted its evangelistic approach to an urban environment as well as the majority of members have adjusted their occupations to the changed culture."

In commenting on the church's need to face the situation they are in, the report points out these factors--the necessity of providing a Christian ministry to the growing number of residents of the county; the fact that the county is over-churched judging from the number of congregations, although underchurched in terms of persons reached by the Gospel; the question of deciding who will organize the new congregations which will appear; facing the long-range implications of population growth (for example, in parts of the county no church has an outstanding Christian education program, yet the public school system has established consolidated plants in the middle of open countryside); the necessity for churches to become again evangelical.

This last is difficult. It is easy to say, "We're here, the door is open, anyone who wants to join is free to come." Such an attitude is incompatible with the New Testament. It is difficult for many well-meaning people to welcome and accept strangers when they come bearing different ideas about how the local church should function. It is also difficult for long-time residents to believe that the county is in the early stages of a period which will see the population increase sevenfold. They may give intellectual assent to this prediction, but it is tempting to make decisions in the local church on the assumption that tomorrow will be little different from yesterday. Some congregations appear to regard the local church as the last enduring tie with the good old days.

The need is clear, but the responsibility for planning rests on the individual congregation. In chapter four we will consider another dimension accompanying urbanization--conflict in values.

For Discussion

1. Near the beginning of chapter 3, this statement is made: "the spirit of fellowship exists as much today, although perhaps in a different quality." How does a congregation measure the quality of their fellowship? Compared to ten years ago, has your congregation scheduled more or fewer occasions for informal gatherings? Why?

2. Does your school system consider the schedule of local churches in their planning (for example, no ball games Wednesday night)? Was this situation different ten years ago?

3. What are signs of affluence in your congregation which were not present five years ago?

4. It is possible for a person to move from country to city and to determinedly become as little involved as possible in the life of the city--and usually no one will question his isolationist position. In church life he will try to keep everything as much as possible like "back home." In the interests of maintaining his standards, is this a justifiable point of view?

1. Bontrager, Edwin, "The Farmer, The Carpenter, The Cabinetmaker" in *Christian Living*, July, 1965.
2. Crysdale, Stewart, *The Changing Church in Canada* (Toronto: United Church of Canada, 1965), pp. 9, 10.
3. Shinn, Roger L., *Tangled World* (New York: Scribner's, 1965), p. 25.
4. Lapp, John E., "Mennonite Homes as I See Them" in *Christian Living*, Sept., 1965.

4 / Confronting Values in Conflict

Alex is a nickname. My real name is W. Alexander Harrison III. Real impressive for a fifteen-year-old, huh? I'll bet you sort of picture me as an average, white, upper-middle-class teenager. But don't let the name fool you. I'm far from upper-middle-class; I'm far from white; and I guess I gotta say it-- I'm far from average. I can see things from an entirely different perspective than the low IQ slum-kid looking up sees them, and I can see things differently from the upper-class high IQ suburban adult looking down sees them.

I aim to ask a few questions to the people who will be reading this book, and let's face it--the only ones who will be reading this are the "looking-downers." I aim to ask them a few questions that I hope will shake them up a little. Okay?

My preacher tells me that God created me. I'll buy that. He also tells me that God loves me. For the sake of the argument, I'll even buy that. Finally, my preacher tells me that this God who created me and loves me, also expects me to obey a few rules and regulations so that I can get to heaven one day.

So first of all, if I want to get to heaven, I'm supposed to honor sweet old mom and dear old dad. Come off it! When I look at her all I feel is digust or pity. When I think of him, all I feel is hate. This God who created me and loves me put me into the situation I'm in, yet He expects me to honor two people who aren't worthy of the slightest bit of respect. If I honor them, I'm a fake, so what I hear Christianity saying to me is, "Be a fake, if you want to get to heaven." Where am I wrong in my thinking--you tell me, huh?

Now let's look at stealing. Have I ever stolen anything? You bet I have! This God who created me and loves me put me into a family where there's no money at all for a so-called allowance. He has me at an age, and He's given me a color skin where I can't find a job, not even a crummy one. So what am I to do for life's necessities? Well, the only answer I can come up with is to make like Robin Hood. I swipe little things from the rich (who won't actually miss them) to give to the poor, namely me. I've taken shoes so I could go to school; clothes for the same reason. Now don't get up on your high horse! I only steal what I absolutely got to have. Yet the Good Book tells me, "Thou shalt not." Okay, what am I to do?

Let's talk yet about coveting. Man, I spend every waking hour doing just that! Maybe if I was like you and yours, and had a nice home, and money to get even a few things, maybe then I'd be satisfied and not have my mouth watering every time I pass a restaurant or a clothing store. But I'm not like you, am I? Am I supposed to pretend I don't want the things you take for granted? Do I have to be a phony, if I want to follow the regulations of this God who created me and loves me? Isn't that what He is asking me to be--a phony? Okay, "Dear Abby," what's the real scoop here?

I've asked you three specific questions, but they are building up to an overall question, that is much more important, and that is simply this. Doesn't God and His love and His regulations actually fit you in your situation better than they do me in mine? I mean, you probably had a mother and a father who were worthy of honor. You probably never *had* to steal. And you probably had enough of the finer things in life so that your tongue wasn't hanging out for everything in sight. So isn't Christianity more for you and your kind than for me and mine? And don't you have to admit that you're asking me to be a phony if I try to follow it?

I've only scratched the surface of the questions I could ask you. But, maybe sometime, when other discussions come up, and you're tempted to give quick and easy answers, maybe you'll remember me. Maybe you'll stop and think, "Sure, that'll work for me, but how about **Alex?**" [1]

In chapter 3 we looked at the facets of urbanization which affect all of us, no matter where we live. As increasing numbers of persons move into highly urbanized situations--the big cities-- they find sharp, abrupt conflicts of their assumed values with the way people around them actually live. Alex has pointed this out dramatically in his story. In this chapter we will look at some of these points of conflict.

"Honor Thy Father and Mother"

Perhaps Alex has said all that needs to be said on this. We have long assumed that one of the clearest ways to teach about God is to compare Him to earthly fathers. What will we tell boys like Alex, who either don't know a father, or if they do, cannot respect him? The church needs to face the implications for millions of families, especially Negro ones, where the father cannot find work, and mother, of necessity, is the provider.

Lyndon B. Johnson, in a speech at Howard University in 1965, said, "Perhaps most important--its influence radiating to every part of life--is the breakdown on the Negro family structure. For this, most of all, white America must accept responsibility. It flows from centuries of oppression and persecution of the Negro man. It flows from the long years of degradation and discrimination which have attacked his dignity and assaulted his ability to provide for his family. . . . Only a minority--less than half--of all **Negro children reach the age of 18 having lived all their lives** with both parents."

One study made of the effects of unemployment on the family, points out that the stages go something like this: credit is exhausted, the wife starts to work, the older children especially

69

resent this change of affairs, the family goes on welfare. At this point, the man may find that two women have taken over his traditional duties--his wife and the social worker. [2]

Although many writers have bemoaned the plight of the family today, it must be pointed out in fairness, that in many ways and cases the family has displayed amazing flexibility in adapting to new situations. What is needed, rather than looking for "what used to be," is an understanding of the nature and needs of family life in today's situation. In the city, where individuals do not depend on relatives and neighbors for support and strength, the role of the family emerges with new significance.

"The Man Who Will Not Work Shall Not Eat."

Statistics on poverty in North America--and around the world, for that matter--are not hard to find. Of concern here is our attitude in the face of these statistics, and our attitude as we actually come into contact with the persons and families who make up the statistics.

Stanley Smucker, an Ohio pastor, has summarized the attitude we too often feel toward the poor. "The church in America represents wealth. The middle- and upper-class people are the 'backbone' of the American church. The poor, then, often become the objects of Christian benevolence. 'You have the poor with you always.' We who are Mennonites often find our attitudes in line with the popular 'do right and you shall prosper' motif.

"But there are some few who reject this deceitful and often misleading idea. Just as Job was not any less righteous in the midst of his poverty, neither are any of 35 million poor Americans unrighteous because they are poor. Sometimes they seem unrighteous to us because they do not accept our middle-class standards.

"Many of these persons lost interest in 'organized righteousness' such as might be found in any highly budgeted, finance-minded congregation. Their tithes are always the lowest, their vacations the shortest, and their family car the oldest. So why try to compete in this free enterprise system of religion?

"Then we wonder. Our missionary efforts to these 'poor' people seem fruitless. We try to help them understand their needs and so we give them things, thinking this will help bring them along the prosperous route. Well, they often do understand! They understand that we have classified them as poor--and our secondhand giveaways are indisputable proof."

Few congregations have faced seriously the implications of the human rights revolution swirling around them. The Negro civil rights struggle is one aspect of it, but we speak here of all Americans who find themselves living in poverty when most of the country lives in affluence. Old ideas about the poor-- that they don't try, or that they are economically necessary, or that poverty makes for spiritual strength--can no longer ease our consciences. A revolutionary conviction is abroad in our land--that poverty is evil and must be eliminated. Where do God's people take hold?

"An Honest Dollar for an Honest Day's Work"

A Mennonite college student went to Chicago for a summer as part of a students-in-industry unit. Eager to learn about life in the city, Susan also wanted to be a Christian witness. One way she could do this was to work hard at her job, no matter how boring and distasteful it was--or so she assumed. She soon discovered that if she did her best, she exceeded the usual speed of the production line, and became immediately the enemy of her co-workers. Many of them had been there for years, and would continue their dull jobs when Susan was back at college.

Susan had grown up in a family that put high value on hard work. The Susans and Sams growing up today face a future in which traditional meanings of work will be completely upset. As the computer and the automated machine are combined, a system of almost unlimited productive capacity results-- cybernation is the word--and greater production with less human labor is the fact.

A work-oriented people, we believe that work is noble and good. One of the problems of automation is that it first takes over the jobs of those persons at the lower end of the work spectrum--the old, the handicapped, the unskilled, the minority groups. If we think of personal dignity in terms of a man's

71

work, and he is often unemployed, or employed at dull, meaningless tasks, where is he to find goals and worth?

"Who Is My Neighbor?"

One of the greatest changes in a move from rural to city life is the difference in relationships with other people. An urban Canadian pastor rather shocked his small-town visitor by saying "I still take people too seriously; in the city you just can't do it." The pastor meant that he had so many contacts each day, lived in the midst of such pressing need, that he had to learn to conserve his emotional responses, or he would be of little help to anyone.

We hear often that in the city a family lived in an apartment for years and didn't know their next-door neighbor. This is unthinkable to a rurally oriented person, accustomed to knowing everyone up and down the road. But no individual can expose himself to all the people he sees in a day's time in the city. Most contacts are brief and impersonal. Being a good neighbor in the apartment may be primarily a matter of being a good tenant, assuming his share of the responsibilities of life in that particular building. Like the Canadian pastor, he needs to select those persons in whose lives he will be more closely involved.

Anonymity has been the target of many critiques of life in the city. An individual may not find identity in his work. He often does not have the identity of a large clan of relatives or of a strong framework of customs and traditions. Perhaps no person or group of persons is concerned for his welfare; his brief contacts with many people lack human warmth. He is anonymous-- unknown. This has contributed to the great sense of loneliness felt by many people in the city. Some congregations have seen this aspect of city life as one of their biggest challenges and opportunities: to provide the place of belonging, the place where the individual, as a child of God, counts and is cared for.

It would not be fair to ignore the other side of the picture-- the fact that for many people, the anonymity of the city provides an exhilarating privacy and freedom, a freedom from the conventions and close scrutiny of small-town life.

"My Father Grew Up in This Church"

Few people today can boast of attending the same church their parents did. One of the words used most often to describe our urban society is mobility. We have discussed the flow of families from rural areas to the city. But this is only part of the story of mobility in American life. Families are on the move within cities as well. Families move in hope of securing better jobs, or they get a better job, then move to a better community.

Each time a family moves, new patterns of life must be worked out. Larry Voth, a Mennonite minister in a Chicago suburb, finds that one of his greatest opportunities is to the families newly moved into the community. Often there are changes which the family has not foreseen, therefore not prepared for--longer commuting distances, no one to baby-sit for the children, higher taxes, little public transportation.

Perhaps this congregation is the exception, for most churches are geared to a stable, long-time-resident population. They are not equipped to move fast enough to reach people as they move in or to follow them when they move out. Large percentages of many church rolls are absentee members. Especially in apartment house areas and in tenement houses, "the Gospel army must be trained to shoot on the wing," as one mission report puts it. [3]

One aspect of mobility is its implications for church leadership. The pastor of Bethel Mennonite Church, located in a Chicago urban renewal area of high-rise apartments, pointed to this as a major problem for the congregation. Those persons who by nature can exert leadership are the first ones to get better jobs and move away. Subsidized housing adds impetus to mobility because when the family income climbs to a certain level, they are automatically evicted. Thus the continual tendency is for the natural leadership of the community to leave it.

The church must use her energy, not to bewail our mobility, but in facing it creatively and positively. The God of the Old Testament was the God of a nomad people, not tied to a particular shrine or hill. Jesus of the New Testament, although intimately involved in the life of particular men in a particular time, ascended--He is forever with us, forever mobile!

73

"Who Am I and Why Am I Here?"

A missionary writes from Japan: "Some of the most interesting hours of the week are spent on Thursday evenings when I have an English class with four young graduate students at Hokkaido University. None of these men embrace any religion seriously. One evening after discussing religions, I asked Mr. Kahata if he didn't feel that he needed 'a faith.' His answer was that for himself he does not feel that he needs one now. This is so typical here in Japan that it almost makes one weep."

And not only in Japan. One of the most baffling aspects of urban society for many of us is the fact that people are simply not asking the questions we expect them to ask. We have assumed that everyone needs "faith" to answer the ultimate questions. The fact is, many people are not asking our "ultimate questions," or are asking in language we do not understand.

A university professor put it this way: "I have no idea what is meant by this introspective and self-centered concept called 'salvation.' I have no interest in being 'saved.' " A question more often on the minds and lips of men today is "Does it work?" Concern with the mysteries of life has been replaced by a concern for the practical and pragmatic.

What does it mean to become God's people in a secular age? Volumes have been written about this, and much in panic. Let us first try to understand more fully what it means to be "secular." Since the industrial revolution of the late eighteenth century, cities are built for and by the commerce and the political structure-- no longer around the cathedral.

In today's industrial city, everything appears to be man-made. "Technology and manufacture make promises and fulfill them. God is mysterious, uncontrollable, unpredictable. But science delivers: this is part of our everyday commonsense experience and none of us escape it. Our children donot doubt that science will one day conquer cancer and send us moonward; we are less sure of the connections between God's promises and the specific forms of their fulfillment." [4]

Perhaps secularization is particularly hard for the church to face and understand because, as Harvey Cox has pointed out,

"The forces of secularization have no serious interest in persecuting religion. Secularization simply bypasses and undercuts religion and goes on to other things. . . . Secularization has accomplished what fire and chain could not: It has convinced the believer that he *could* be wrong, and persuaded the devotee that there are more important things than dying for the faith. The gods of traditional religions live on as private fetishes or the patrons of congenial groups, but they play no part whatever in the public life of the secular metropolis."[5]

Becoming God's People Today--in these first four chapters we have focused primarily on "today," on assessing our situation. Now we turn more specifically to our resources and guidelines. As we consider God's work in His world we discover anew our task and our resources for facing life in our day.

For Discussion

1. Have you ever met anyone like Alex? How many people like Alex would your community provide if it were in the inner city?

2. When young people from your congregation have gone into a city situation, such as VS, I-W or a university, have they been prepared for their new experiences?

3. If yours is a city congregation, look at the question from the other side. As you observe individuals and families move from small towns to the city, what have they contributed to the life of your congregation? In what ways has their adjustment been difficult?

4. Considering a congregation in a rural community and one in a large city, are there more differences or more factors in common, and what would be some of each?

---

1. Finlaw, William W., in an address to the Editors of Church Magazines for Children and Youth, April, 1964 (St. Louis, Mo.). Mr. Finlaw is Protestant Chaplain to the juvenile court and related institutions in St. Louis. W. Alexander Harrison III does not exist, yet he lives in thousands of youth like him.
2. "Full Equality for Negroes" in *Current*, Nov., 1965, p. 10.
3. Miller, Kenneth, *Man and God in the City* (New York: Friendship Press, 1965), p. 43.
4. Marty, Martin, *Babylon by Choice* (New York: Friendship Press, 1965), p. 55.
5. Cox, Harvey, *The Secular City* (New York: Macmillan, 1965), p. 2.

5 / Joining God in His World

What has happened at Christ Church, Presbyterian, in Burlington, Vermont, did not come about as the result of a strategy. Each of the three directions pursued came as a gift and seemed in its turn to be "the" answer which would sew everything together. However, as each was modified by the next, the result was that all three experiences have taught us something about the church as the body of Christ called to His mission in the world.

Rather than erecting a building to bring people inside the church walls, we started on the premise that persons should first know the basic mission of the church. Our major thrust became: "How can the church be a people faithful to Jesus Christ in this city?"

On completing the six-months' membership class, adults were encouraged to continue their study in special-interest groups. Many groups were started, and many failed. Gradually, we worked out a more disciplined program which now includes a two-hour Bible study on Sunday night and a study of ethics in occupations. Although study proved not to be "the" answer, it set the stage for the next development.

One cannot study God's mission without being engaged in the issues and perplexities of his world. A couples group, after studying the servant passages in Isaiah, was moved to make weekly visits to the county jail and report back to the congregation on Sundays. Sometimes they visited families of the prisoners, their former employees, or their attorneys, on behalf of the inmates. It became a ministry of reconciliation. A university group was led to open a coffeehouse on the campus to discuss current issues in the light of the Christian faith.

Because of a growing concern about the use of leisure time, another coffeehouse combined with a bookstore was established on the main business street. The Loft is open six nights a week from seven to midnight. Six different teams of volunteers, who meet monthly for study, operate it, doing everything from waiting on tables to putting on programs. As a church-sponsored enterprise, the Loft is, first, a meeting place for neighbors and strangers, including the sick, the lonely, and the social outcasts; second, a missionary presence, awake to people's situation; and third, a place of witness in the midst of burning issues.

Pushed outside our own walls and ourselves, we learned that the stranger in whom Christ confronts us is "out there," where the locus of God's mission of peace is. To meet him in the worlds of crisis and alienation, we first had to risk going "out there." Prison visists led participants into a citywide survey of public health conditions, to take positions on political issues, and publicize them. Serving in the coffee shop helped students think through basic questions of life. Missionary work at the Loft impressed on volunteers the need to articulate their faith when asked, "Why are you here?"

The undertaking which is engaging our current efforts is *God's mission* in the world into which the whole church is called. A section of a letter from the official board to the congregation reads: "It has been proposed that, in order for this church to be truly in, but not of, the world; to be free of self-centeredness and to be, in fact, a community bound only to God, we dispose of all our property and buildings at 915 North Avenue." What we do about this suggestion has not yet been decided, but with the emphasis now on God's work in the world, Christ Church has the task of trying to discover where that beginning point might be and risk the going. [1]

When God commissioned man to take charge of world affairs from Eden, He set in motion a chain reaction which yet continues to affect human life on this planet and beyond. The interval was short, however, until the quiet glory of the garden as the hub of activity was exchanged for the confusion of Cain's city and Babel's skyscraper.

Abram, though, was asked to leave the urban scene in Haran and move out toward an unknown rural situation. The Pentateuch reports the gypsy-like journeyings of God's people Israel toward Canaan, the land of promise and potential. In fact, in one way or another, the entire Old Testament is the record of how God acted through a community of faithful followers. Finally the New Israel which gathered after Pentecost was recognized as a people for God's own possession. (See I Peter 2:9, 10.)

In the New Testament, particularly the **Book** of Acts, the continuing story of the people of God is detailed, noting both the faith and the life of the early Christians. But by the last half of the twentieth century so much hedge has grown up around the entity labeled *church* and the vines cling so tenaciously to the structure called *church* that a candid exposure picturing the real thing is almost impossible to observe.

Our first task then is to try to chop the hedge and pull off the vines in order to discern the essence of the church. A careful consideration of the New Testament record will afford our best clues.

To Discuss the Essence

The English word *church* is generally derived from a Greek word meaning "The Lord's house" but it never occurs in this sense in the New Testament because the early Christians did not use buildings for worship until long after the New Testament was written. *Church* is used in the New Testament, rather, to translate the Greek word *ekklesia*--an assembly or gathering of human beings; it covers the twin aspects of coming and being together. The same word is used in the Septuagint (the Greek Old Testament) to translate a Hebrew word meaning "congregation" or "assembly" thus indicating that at least for 200 years before Christ this was a common term to designate God's people.

The common Greek word for *church* appears 115 times in the New Testament and refers to both local gatherings and the general, or universal, body of Christ's followers. That *ekklesia* has to do with people rather than buildings or organizations is abundantly clear.

A second Greek word with which we need to become familiar to understand the full New Testament meaning of church is *koinonia* or *fellowship*--the word suggests joint participation and mutuality. To be a part of *ekklesia* implies participation in *koinonia* and true church becomes true fellowship.

Perhaps the simplest description of the New Testament church is contained in Jesus' words in Matthew 18:20: "For where two or three have met together in my name, I am there among them." As Erland Waltner has summarized so succinctly, "the church is where Christ is living and reigning in the midst of His gathered people." In *These Are My People*, a study of the New Testament understanding of the church, Harold S. Bender called to attention three different but related ways of looking at the church. To these we now look briefly.

The Church as the People of God

The New Testament word *ekklesia* deliberately identifies the New Testament church as the people of God in the same stream as God's faithful in the Old Testament and before Pentecost. A given historic group stands in such a relationship to God as to belong to Him as His people.

As the people of God were gathered together in a special way by God's mighty acts in Egypt and Sinai so the new people of God were constituted by God's mighty acts in Jesus Christ. By referring to the church as the people of God we thus draw attention to redemption/salvation history and God's mighty works at the climax.

The Church as the Body of Christ

Another image, the body of Christ, emphasizes the immediate relation and centrality of Christ to the church. Since the resurrection the life of the church is to be understood as wholly dependent upon Christ, as the living human body is dependent upon a source of life outside of itself. Behind the image of the body is the Hebrew notion of corporate personality. For the Hebrew, the individual existed only as a particular expression of the total people.

The body of Christ is a picture of God's act in Christ, of Christ's coming to give Himself for us so we can be one with Him in order that we may receive all that God has to give us. "For it is in Christ that the complete being of the Godhead dwells embodied, and in him you have been brought to completion" (Colossians 2:9). The acts of God and Christ, together with our response, produce the body of Christ since our personal central decision of faith identifies us with all other sinners who have made the same decision.

The Church as the Holy Community

The most expressive New Testament word for the common experience which marks the people of God is the word *koinonia*-- a participation in something in which others also participate, a conscious sharing with someone else in a joint possession on a continuing basis.

Members of the Christian community are all sons of a common Father. All share in an undivided Christ and an undivided Holy Spirit. All are members one of another. It is in this sense that the church is not an organization but an organism. It results from life, not from planned agreement. Believers in Christ do not decide to *have* fellowship or to become a community--they are, by nature, a community.

True Christian community is created and carried by the awareness of a common body of beliefs, a common life in Christ, a common commitment to Him in faith and obedience, and a common expression of Christian love. This awareness must be communicated by the witness of members to each other and by mutual admonition to obey and to act. Members in the holy community submit to and take binding action for each other. Ethical decision is made in the context of the church where Christ is the Head.

Two or Three Sharing God's Mission

The church is made up of those called-out people who respond to God, those who come into life by repentance and faith. The church is the company of God's people living in the world in time and in space--visible, identifiable, human. When and where two or three are gathered in Christ's name to celebrate the Lord's Supper and baptize those reconciled to Christ and man, to study the Scripture, to take binding action for each other, to respond to need in the world--this is *church*.

If we recognize that to be the church means sharing in God's mission we will need to be involved in places, and identified with people in the urban world from which our rural past has allowed us to remain neatly separated. This means that the church exists for the world, rather than for herself.

"I Gave the World a Farewell Look"

Christians have not always focused their worldly mission so emphatically, however. When Menno Simons wrote his first hymn about 1540 he expressed a common view of the world which many believers have held both before and since that time:

When I turned me to the Lord
I gave the world a farewell look.

Menno underscored his viewpoint by emphasizing in a letter of instruction on discipline to the Franeker church in Friesland fifteen years later: "Remember that you are the Lord's people, separated from the world." According to the *Mennonite Encyclopedia* the label *worldliness* has historically been common among Mennonites. The term has been used to "designate attitudes, tendencies, and behavior influenced by the 'world,' thought of as the evil system of life and conduct as opposed to Christ." But a major difficulty has been to identify precisely what the world is.

82

Society Organized Without God

The development of the word in the New Testament can be traced quite naturally beginning with its meaning merely a physical system and then the abode of man--that order of which man is the center, and within which the human family moves. A natural next step was to use the word to actually denote mankind within that order. And finally, world comes to mean that order of things alienated from God--human beings separated from, and acting in opposition to Him. Or, as William Barclay put it, "Human society organizing itself without God." The world, therefore, according to the New Testament, stands in need of judgment, and redemption.

Into just this kind of world Christ's followers are sent. In His prayer on the eve before He suffered, Jesus reaffirmed His commission, "As thou hast sent me into the world, I have sent them into the world" (John 17:18). Into the world, not to be engulfed by the world but to be light and salt--light which is still radiant, salt which is still seasoned. But if salt is to change the potatoes it must get from the shaker into the saucepan. And if light is to displace darkness it must be turned on. Jesus sends His disciples into the world to lead the world back to God.

Principalities and Powers

At this point it is needful to view the world from another New Testament perspective--a consideration of Christ and *powers*. Paul frequently mentions powers, principalities, dominions (see Romans 13:1, Ephesians 3:10; 6:2; Colossians 1:16; 2:15). Until about the time of World War I powers meant something invisible and spooky. But the meaning became more concrete as the word was applied to nations and their military might. We now have come to understand that powers are all the varying impersonal forces which rule society--economy, sex, religion, prejudice, nationalism, militarism--all those things which influence and often dominate our lives without being fully visible.

In every realm of life the powers--politics, class, national interest, accepted morality, for example--unify men, yet separate men from God, H. Berkhof has pointed out in *Christ and the Powers*. "Yet precisely by giving unity and direction they separate these many lives from the true God; they let us believe that we have found the meaning of existence, whereas they really estrange us from true meaning."

Powers and principalities are not figments of imagination but living realities God uses for His own good pleasure. They are the framework of creation which prevent disintegration, the dike which prevents a chaotic flood from submerging an alienated world. By keeping men alive and in check, powers thus serve a positive function, yet their demonic potential dare never be minimized.

Christ Frees from the Powers

When a man is redeemed by Christ he is freed from slavery to the powers. When Jesus defeated principalities and powers we mean not that they were demolished but that they no longer grip men. Rather, men have the power and responsibility to rule over them and use them responsibly before God. By her existence the church demonstrates that men can live free from the powers, and proclaims to the powers that their unbroken dominion has ended. The people of God are liberated to participate in God's action in the world.

Anxiety gives way to carefulness since the future lies with God. In faith we accept that all God has created is good. Before the eye of faith the Holy Spirit shrinks the powers. Believers do not flee the world, but avoid bowing down to anything in it as a god.

Albert H. van den Heuvel, a young Dutch minister, has well summarized the relation of the powers to God's mission in *These Rebellious Powers*. "The evil nature of the powers became clear when God Himself became man; the powers tried to put Him aside and finally crucified Him. They thus gave proof of their rebellion against God. But Jesus, in reconciling them to the Father on the cross, put them back where they belonged, namely in His own victory parade, where they are openly recognizable as servants rather than masters."

In spite of its ambiguities and contradictions, the world is God's creation. Involvement is God's way of relating to the world. He sent His Son *into* the world. The world is the sphere in which we serve God's redemptive purposes--God's created world is man's

84

meeting place with man. The question for the people of God is not whether to become involved in the world, but how.

Implications for Moving Ahead

In this chapter we have noted that *church* in its basic meaning has to do with people rather than buildings or meetings or organizations. The church is the becoming of people under God to do God's work in the world as the body of Christ and the community of the Spirit. We have looked at the meaning of the *world* into which God sent His people to be His representatives. We have noted that as those freed by Christ from the powers, God's people are called to be involved in the life of the world working continually to unmask the powers.

A young Japanese theologian has aptly characterized the concept of mission which Americans export to the Orient as removing fish from a dirty river called the world and placing them in a clean pool called the church. Hopefully, this chapter has sharpened the Biblical understanding that both world and church are God's creation-- we can distinguish between them, but dare not separate them from one another. The Christian stands in the midst of the world to minister to the world. The question which we now must face is what should be the posture of the people of God as they are placed in the world by God to be His instrument of mission?

For Discussion

1. Clarify the New Testament meaning of *church*
2. Describe briefly the church as (a) the people of God; (b) the body of Christ; and (c) the holy community.
3. Summarize in your own words a definition of the church based on your study of this chapter.
4. Clarify the New Testament meaning of *world*.
5. What are principalities and powers? In what ways are they good? In what ways are they demonic? How should Christians relate to the powers?

---

1. Abridged from Hollister, William H., "The Church 'Out There' " in *International Journal of Religious Education*, Sept., 1965.

6 / Accepting the City
as God's Gift

When the East Harlem Protestant Parish was started 17 years ago, we simply tried to reproduce the patterns of the church as we had known them and as we had been instructed at seminary. Putting it bluntly, we got clobbered.

The kind of sermons we tried to preach, full of literary allusions, didn't ring any bells. But worst of all was the Sunday-school literature. We tried everything from one end of the theological spectrum to the other. And this is what we discovered: Sunday-school materials from all denominations have the same underlying presupposition: if you want to teach Johnny about Jesus, he has to live in a family where he is loved. Then we can explain that God is like a father and the love of Jesus is like the love you know at home.

We had a rough time in Harlem for quite a while, because the twentieth-century Protestant church is not equipped to meet the challenge of the urban world. Neither our ecclesiastical structures nor our Christian approach is geared to the needs of the city. The truth is that most Protestants don't like cities. Look at New York City, for example. If everybody in the five boroughs of New York City were put into a religious pigeonhole, about 50 percent would be Catholic, about 30 percent would be Jewish and less than 20 percent would be Protestant, of whom over half would be Negro. Since half of the white Protestants are not connected with any church, this means that less than five percent of the 8.5 million people of New York City are white Protestants.

We have evacuated from New York City and most other cities as though they had the plague. Most denominational literature assumes that the city is an evil place and must be attacked from outside. Heaven help you if you have to live in it and share its destiny. This assumption that God is not at work in the city is a denial of Biblical faith. God, the Lord of history, seems to be putting people in cities to live. God is the Lord of the cities as well as the Lord of the countryside.

When the East Harlem Protestant Parish began, we who were white, middle-class, theologically trained ministers looked over the city as outsiders. But we had trouble communicating with the people whom we were attempting to help. So we hired a brilliant research girl to study East Harlem, to live with the people and find out what made them tick, in order that we might learn how to communicate with them.

After six months she came back and told us, "This is the phoniest enterprise I've ever been associated with. The problem is not the people of East Harlem; the problem is not in your lack of understanding their life and culture. The problem is you. You are trying to be professionals, and you are not willing to be human beings sharing the common life of the neighborhood."

We had been failing to take the incarnation seriously. Christ did not set Himself up as apart from mankind. He walked the dusty roads of Palestine and shared the common life. We had been a bunch of phonies. We had been standing on the bank of East Harlem watching the flood tide of human life sweep by, analyzing it, dissecting it, writing articles about it, but unwilling to get personally involved. [1]

*T*he world in which God's people--the church--find themselves today is an urban world, a world of cities--city bustle, city ideas, city ways of doing things. The idea sparking this chapter comes from a recent paperback: *The City--God's Gift to the Church.* The Presbyterian city evangelists who wrote the book out of firsthand attempts to be the people of God in the city, have clarified how the city may be thought of as the bearer of gifts to the church.

● The city brings the church face to face with its own failures and with the needs and despair of men who live without Christ.

● The city forces the church to see that there is no new life apart from the love of Christ and apart from men and women who share this love in their lives.

● The city demands that the church seek both new and old patterns of witness which may once more make known in the world and in the church the lordship of Jesus Christ.

In this chapter we shall look at illustrative ways in which groups of Christians accepted God's gifts of the city and attempted to become His people in their *being* and in their *doing.*

New Circumstances May Demand New Ways

New circumstances may well demand new ways of doing things. When Christians take both the world and the church seriously something is bound to change. That change, though, must be made deliberately and consciously. New ways of doing things must actually reflect new understanding and new commitment--not newness for the sake of novelty. The city context offers the Christian community ample opportunity to experiment in becoming the people of God. Such experimentation requires flexibility and adaptability--a willingness to forge ahead into uncharted areas with a kind of purposeful recklessnes. Experimentation may unsettle the person who seeks ready-made answers before discerning the real questions. It also unsettles the person who is confident that the way in which something has or hasn't been done for the past quarter century is the once-for-all-time anointed way. Nonetheless the experimentation must go on.

As long ago as ten years, a sociologist at a conference on cultural problems asserted, "Mennonites must be told simply and bluntly: not everything that is rural is for that reason Christian." In an October, 1965, interview, a Mennonite missions leader underscored this same point. "Given the living Gospel, with the Holy Spirit as its chief authority, we are bound to communicate this message by all means within our power. But no one evangelistic approach, either at home or abroad, dare be considered either a necessarily permanent one, nor yet as a cure-all for the church's impotence in witnessing. The Holy Spirit is not limited to a few ways of working, nor is He obliged to honor forever some methods that might have had their seasons and appropriate days." [2]

"To build Christ's church in the modern city demands that we must go beyond the traditional church patterns," Chicago pastor Harry Spaeth summarized during an informal discussion of urban concerns. The urban situation of the mid-twentieth century, according to Sociologist Paul Peachey, calls for "a readiness to accept a completely different pattern of church life from what we now know. It is not that someone will luckily succeed in devising a new blueprint, but rather that Christians enter with greater freedom and immediacy into the structures of urban life, prepared to walk the way that will open to them." [3]

Beyond Traditional Church Patterns

As faithfulness in the world is stressed new directions are being pursued; new forms of witness are emerging. Experimentation at Christ Church, Presbyterian, Burlington, Vermont, was reported at the beginning of chapter 5. The moving story of The Church of the Savior, Washington, D.C., is detailed in Elizabeth O'Conner's book, *Call to Commitment*. First Methodist Church, Germantown, Pa., is another example of real congregational struggle to face creatively the call of God in a city situation. Each of these three congregations has found a coffeehouse useful in its mission.

By mid-1965 there were over 200 non-commercial coffeehouses in 42 states either sponsored by churches or having direct religious affiliation. A study of the movement by the Protestant chaplain of the University of Vermont projected the coffeehouses as one example of "the kind of evangelism the churches must undertake to be effective today." The study, reported in *Interchurch News* (November, 1965), found that many such houses cross racial, cultural, and religious lines without fanfare. Discussion and entertainment stress the strong theological content of contemporary drama, poetry, and folk music.

In the Gaslight Square district of St. Louis, The Exit, according to the menu, "is a place for people to gather and talk over a cup of coffee. It is a place for real conversation and for real listening." Also in St. Louis, and taking its cue from The Exit, The Circle in the Mill Creek redevelopment area, is both a coffee-house and a bookshop. The pastor of the sponsoring church told a news reporter, "It is important to individual Christians and to churches that they get out and listen to others as well as talk about their faith."

On Chicago's South Side, the Woodlawn Mennonite Church staffs the Quiet Place--an effort to bring the church into the marketplace. Former overseas missionary Marie J. Regier now finds the Quiet Place an effective field for mission as she pours coffee. "People from many professions and a variety of beliefs come into our coffee shop and bookstore. We learn many things about them, including their coffee-drinking habits. We find many times when we can say, 'Yes, this store is sponsored by the church.' And to people's questions we can answer with what our church believes. Sometimes I explain that the workers are mostly volunteers. This is not a money-making institution. It is here in order to get in touch with the people in the community. We know that there are some who have come into our church through the contact at the Quiet Place. But we are not just out to get members. If persons can feel the breath of God in the Quiet Place, we are satisfied." [4]

The examples just reported should not be taken to mean that every congregation wanting to move ahead in mission must set up a coffeehouse. What such examples do mean, however, is that every congregation of God's people needs to be alert to new settings for Christian witness.

A Setting for Building Relationships

Similar in purpose to a coffeehouse, but of a quite different nature, is the Glad Tidings Sandwich Shop in New York City. Launched by the Glad Tidings Mennonite congregation in late 1964, the shop bustles from 7 a.m. until 10 p.m. with "all sizes and shapes of children, workmen, and teenagers." The store is far more than a business risk or an energy consumer. It is a setting for building relationships. It is a means of piercing the barrier of unfamiliarity built between distrustful city dwellers. It is a place to "rub off" Christ.

Pastor Paul Burkholder explained the purpose. "We were looking for a giving experience that would not mechanize our witnessing by doing it for us. We searched for a program that would not isolate Christianity from our community. The store creates a setting in which we can give ourselves."

During the school year dozens of children from Alexander Burger Junior High School across the street pile into the shop for lunch and snacks. Three attendants are kept hopping from freezer to counter during the hour before noon.

The excitement and pain of this venture is involvement with people. The program becomes secondary when Christ's love reaches out through human flesh and blood and penetrates hate, loneliness, and rejection. Flying bottles and cutting curses demand divine concern; any superficial toleration or phony nicety crumbles under the pressure. The Glad Tidings Sandwich Shop continues to pulsate with people--people filled with hate and loneliness confronting a team of Christ-filled workers. VS-er Leon Stauffer verbalized their united concern, "The love of Christ must be ours before it can become theirs." [5]

Inner City Parish Ventures

Another type of urban faithfulness is illustrated in the inner city parish ventures such as New York's East Harlem Protestant

Parish described at the beginning of this chapter. East Harlem began as an experiment by three seminary students who, with the help of community young people, renovated a storefront as a base of operations. In the seventeen ensuing years Christians from many denominations have attempted (using the words of the book title by one of the originating sparks) to be *God's Colony in Man's World*.

In Chicago the West Side Christian Parish began in 1952 with one small storefront church close to the busy corner of Roosevelt and Ashland. From the beginning, the centers of Parish activity have deliberately been placed in accessible storefront buildings, near where the people live. There has been much expansion since the early days. The first congregation has grown in strength and numbers. Two other congregations, a technical assistance office, and special project centers have been set up. Although each congregation has developed in differing ways, neighborhood witness is coordinated.

Men and women of various talents have joined in the venture. A team approach and a common or unified strategy have characterized the work of the Parish from its earliest days. A group ministry was formed, made up of the long-term, full-time staff members, bound together at the outset by common disciplines in the matters of vocations, salary, group religious life, and civic participation. Each minister lives in the community where he works, and each participates actively in community affairs.

A Parish brochure concluded, "The vision and hope of the West Side Christian Parish has not been the building of mighty Gothic churches and vast congregations. No, it has been a vision of inducing men to be men, of calling city people to be, in fact and in truth, what they are--children loved by God."

To Bring Religion into Everyday Life

Yet another ecumenical approach to inner city church outreach is the Near North Side Team Ministry in St. Louis initiated in the fall of 1964. Four pastors--a Baptist, an Episcopalian, a Methodist and a Presbyterian--and a Mennonite secretary work primarily in the Pruitt-Igoe public housing project where nearly

12,000 persons live in 33 eleven-story buildings within an area slightly smaller than five city blocks. *The Housing Digest*, published by the St. Louis Housing Authority, announced in a front-page article, "The Team Ministry approach to religion is a fairly new idea among the churches. It is an attempt to bring religion into everyday life and activities. The Team Ministry hope to serve the community in all areas to talk to them about their problems."

One of the Pruitt-Igoe apartments converted into an unimposing office suite is Team headquarters. Their ministry is personal rather than formal. Through regular and systematic apartment calling they learn to know and befriend community residents. Eight adult Bible study classes are held in apartments of tenants. Two pre-kindergarten classes use religious subject matter. A Saturday afternoon children's art class and a youth choir rehearsal both include religious instruction. Emergency assistance takes team ministers into local courts, hospitals, fire scenes. One pastor is on duty until midnight four evenings each week. A major thrust of the Team witness is expressed through cooperation with area social and religious ministries.

Three blocks from the Pruitt-Igoe project the Bethesda Mennonite Church seeks to serve alongside the Near Northside Team Ministry. Although not a formal member of the Team Ministry, Pastor Swartzentruber works closely with the team ministers both in determining strategy and serving needs. When Hubert and June Swartzentruber first went to St. Louis, they set up housekeeping in a ninth floor Pruitt-Igoe apartment. Bethesda Church, which now touches perhaps 500 lives each year and has a stable membership of about one-tenth that number, was actually conceived in that apartment through cell-group evangelism.

In the crowds of the inner city, many are lost. They know no one, they live alone, they see only the delivery boy or the coalman when he delivers the goods and stays only long enough to collect his pay. No one to talk to, no one to care! Mr. Gaines was a lonesome old man who wandered the streets. But he was found by Christians at Bethesda where he discovered his identity in the church. He still has no relatives, but he has those who care. He uses the church address as his own and is proud of his relationship with God and His people.

About 275 miles north of St. Louis, another Mennonite pastor is guiding a congregation in becoming the people of God in the Chicago suburban community of Markham, Illinois. Many of the social issues facing the church in the inner city of St. Louis are the same concerns which confront suburban Southwest Chicago.

Driving down the street with the pastor of the community Mennonite Church, we would never have guessed the amount of fear, hatred, and heartache the "For Sale" signs represented. As quietly and as quickly as the appearance of dandelions in springtime, the signs had appeared. By June of 1965, 40 of the some 700 homes in this area were occupied by Negro families and the Markham Mennonite congregation was immersed in a ministry of reconciliation in this tense and explosive situation.

"We really put the Spirit to the test," remarked Pastor Larry Voth, "when we welcomed into our membership persons from other races." Some members felt that for the first time, the church was in reality being the church. Other members opposed integration so strongly that they withdrew from the fellowship of the congregation. One lady left the church, promising to pray every day and search the Scriptures specifically for God's leading in this question; in three months she returned to the congregation.

Motivation for beginning the congregation in 1955 came largely from concern for Mennonite families moving from the two General Conference Mennonite inner city churches. Coupled with this concern was a desire to establish a witness in a relatively "unchurched" area, and this purpose has been realized more fully than the first one, according to Pastor Voth. Organized with 18 charter members in 1957, the membership in 1965 included 47 adults, with over 200 persons participating in various phases of the life of the congregation. The congregation completed their church building in 1959.

Markham believes that its most fruitful evangelistic thrust is through the parents of families in the community. In September, 1964, the congregation opened a day nursery, licensed by the state to care for 23 children. The congregation was instrumental in securing the services of two Mennonite college graduates who are hired by the city as fulltime youth workers. Good newspaper coverage has made the city aware of the presence of Mennonites in Markham.

While involvement in community needs has drawn the congregation to a deeper life together (as evidenced in renewed interest in midweek meeting), the Markham congregation is not without its problems. Some of these are irregularity of work schedules and attendance at church, inactive members, and the financial problems posed by the fact that most suburban families are struggling with heavy personal debts.

In reply to the question, "Does being a Mennonite seem to help or hinder your witness in the city?" Pastor Voth's answer was enthusiastic and unhesitating. "One of the most exciting moments of my life comes every time I can knock on a door and introduce myself as the pastor of the local Mennonite congregation. Because this usually raises a question, it is easy to explain that we are a New Testament church that is trying to discover what God is saying in the twentieth century."

To discover what God is saying to His people in century 20--this task drives the church to accept gladly but seriously the city as today's setting for mission. In chapter seven we look at the particular place, both past and present, of Mennonites in the city.

For Discussion

1. How may the city be thought of as a gift of God to the church?

2. Have there been suggestions in your congregation to experiment with new ways of doing things but the suggestions were thwarted because some persons were satisfied with the old ways?

3. What are the cautions to note in connection with experimenting with new church patterns?

4. Evaluate some of the ventures in faithfulness reported in this chapter. What are their strong points? Their weak points?

1. Webber, George, "The City Needs a New Kind of Church" in *Eternity*, Aug., 1965.
2. Mosemann, John H., "Where Are We Going in Missions?" in *Gospel Herald*, Oct. 26, 1965.
3. Peachey, Paul, *The Church in the City* (Newton: Faith and Life Press, 1963), p. 101.
4. Regier, Marie J., "Visitors to the Quiet Place," in *The Mennonite*, Nov. 16, 1965).
5. Hoover, Ruth, in *Missionary Messenger*, Dec., 1965.

7 / Reviewing Our Heritage

What Is the Mennonite Church in the City?
It is many things.
Sometimes and in some places it is this; sometimes and in some
   places it is that.

It is a church awakening to a vision, still rubbing the sleep from
   its soul.
It is a church being lulled into slumber, entranced by immersion
   into the affluent society.

It is hungering and thirsting men and women feeding on the
   Living Bread.
It is satisfied people who know not that they are starving,
   zealously guarding stale crusts in decorated boxes.

It is conviction and confusion, revival and rebellion and renewal,
   compromise and courage.
It is a young church, sometimes robust with high ideals and
   daring vision, and sometimes sick with adolescent self-
   centeredness.
It is a church in middle-age, sometimes creatively mature and
   sometimes prematurely senile.

99

It is a pious church, priding itself on its absence of drinkers and dancers;

and sometimes it is a Christian church, seeking to redeem both the piously proud and the proudly sophisticated.

It is a church conformed to noncomformity,
and sometimes conformed to not conform to nonconformity;
and sometimes a church transformed by God, conformed to Christ.
It is a church sometimes desperately concerned about saving itself,
and sometimes a church finding itself as it concentrates on following its Lord.

It is a church of many meetings and occasional encounters;
a church of persons engaged in a dynamic program of pilgrimage,
and sometimes a church of programs shackling the upward pilgrimage of persons.

It is a church extending a hand "in the name of Christ" to the brother across the sea;

and sometimes isolating itself from the brother across the street.
It is a congenial church, offering friendship to all who enter its doors,

and sometimes an exclusive church, subtly conscious of who is "our kind."

It is a church of prodigal sons leaving the Father's house, with some returning to the Father;

and a church of older brothers, jealous of the Father's prodigal love.

It is a part of the Church Universal, which Christ loves and for which He gave His life.

It is a part of the Church Universal, which some love today, and for which they are giving their life.

It is a part of the body of Christ, sometimes amputating itself from the larger body and sometimes groping to work in harmony with the other members.

It is a church with prophetic voices calling for renewal;
It is a church with priestly voices calling for peace;
It is a church seeking to hear the voice of the Lord above the
  voices of men. [1]

"*T*he big city," according to New York City's John Smucker,
"is God's greatest gift to the American Mennonite church in this
generation. The city's challenge is producing new life in the church.
Vibrant, convinced, New Testament Anabaptist Christians belong
to our urban Mennonite churches. Mennonites can love the city,
they must, if they are Christian."

In chapter 6 we observed ways in which God's people in
such places as St. Louis, Missouri, and Markham, Illinois, have
accepted and used the gifts of the city to become the *church* in
the *world*. We turn at this point to look more self-consciously
at the family of Christians who call themselves Mennonites and
their record in relationship to the urban scene.

One historical study showing the overwhelmingly urban
background of the early Anabaptists, concluded that initially
Anabaptism was an urban movement with both the rate of physical
mobility and occupational transfer being comparatively high. [2]

Although the life of our Anabaptist forebears pulsated in the
urban areas of Europe--Zurich, Bern, Strasburg, Augsburg,
Amsterdam, Harlem, Danzig, Emden--the sixteenth-century believers' church moved quickly to a rural viewpoint. Four major
factors in this development stand out.

Reasons for Rural Switch

1. Severe persecutions drove the Mennonites into early rural
exile. Through their pioneer agricultural efforts in Switzerland,
eastern France, southern Germany, Prussia, and Russia they
eventually gained limited tolerance and similarly their reputation
as farmers made them desirable immigrants in the New World.

2. Mennonites entered America by the rural frontier and

settled almost exclusively in self-sustaining agrarian communities. This in contrast to other denominations who at least had an urban minority and a professional clergy to keep them in touch with the city.

3. Encounter with the new culture heightened the ethnic solidarity of the Mennonite community. Despite good neighborly cooperation, a strong "we-they" consciousness developed.

4. The traditional Anabaptist understanding of church and world as two distinct entities strengthened the rural mind-set and delayed absorption into the general culture.

World War II Turns the Tide

While the urbanization of American Mennonites yet lags behind the urbanization of the general population, the gap between the two is rapidly narrowing, as we observed in chapter 1.

World War II, Paul Peachey has emphasized, forms a distinct watershed in Mennonite city attitudes and relations. Abruptly thousands of young Mennonites were scattered through Civilian Public Service into what was often their first urban experience. Hundreds participated in overseas relief projects after the war. Postwar conscription linked with increasing voluntary service to carry the following generation further into the urban scene. College attendance, in both church and private institutions, mushroomed. Tentacles from metropolis engulfed rural communities. "In sum," Peachey concluded, "Mennonites entered the city, and it can be said with some legitimacy, the city entered Mennonites." [3]

Thus by 1951 a Mennonite mission board executive secretary wrote in his annual report that the city is "where our traditional and rural Mennonite way of life is most strongly challenged to adapt itself to an urban culture. The problems in this are in some cases severe but we dare not shrink from them because the Gospel is for all men in every culture."

And by 1965 a college student, after a Christmas vacation VS project in Cleveland, summarized his feelings this way: "The project seemed to be more than educational--it was motivating. I don't really feel I'll be satisfied living anywhere but in the city. This is where the people are moving. The church is slow and

102

often irrelevant. Most of all here are people who can help me and who need help. Perhaps I can help make the church relevant to transient neighborhoods--perhaps knock down psychological spiritual walls between people and ultimately introduce them to Jesus Christ."

But Not All Convinced

But there were dissonant voices along the way. A 1940 thesis suggested that Mennonite funds used for city outreach might better be used to establish young people on farms so they wouldn't need to look for work in cities. [4] Many Mennonites continue in the rural tradition which reflects a skeptical image of city life well described by St. Louis pastor Hubert Swartzentruber:

"We tend to look with some misgiving on these giant centers of self-made mountains of steel and concrete, and flashing lights and bustling traffic. We often see only the madness and loose morals, the murder, robbery, dope addiction, the police wrestling with the gangs, the taverns, and the prostitutes.

"We wonder about the bulging welfare roles and the tired social workers, the extremely rich and the extremely poor, the unjust landlords and the ungrateful tenants, the power structures and the ghettos, the pawn shops and loan companies, the high interest rates and low income."

World in Capsule

From Cleveland, Pastor Vern Miller had this to add. "Perhaps the city is repulsive to some because it is our present world in capsule form. Most major metropolitan areas have a bit of every human and environmental phenomenon on the earth. We can live comfortably in our world if we don't have to constantly see it close up, but to be confronted with its totality every day can be depressing frustrating. This is what God experiences every moment! We must ask how long we can hide our eyes from reality by burying our heads in the soil of rural America.

"For too long the church has arrogantly stooped to help the downtrodden, the poorly educated, the culturally deprived, and the spiritually starved urban dweller. When will we learn that charity is not the answer so long as we covertly support the *status quo?* The great challenge of the city is to identify with its people as Christ did in Jerusalem. Not until their hurt becomes our hurt; their social frustration our discontent with society; their poverty our efforts to seek legal redress in their behalf; their spiritual need our genuine concern for their total discomfort will Christ become real in urban racial ghettos. For it is only when men are reconciled to each other that Christianity becomes real!"

Reconciliation Effected in Atlanta

Pastor Elvin Martin has provided an apt illustration from Atlanta showing how Christianity became real as the people of God lived God's love amid hate, envy, and strife. The Atlanta fellowship includes 13 Negro and 12 white members. "One of our members works under a Christian supervisor who became furious when he heard that Carl was going to an interracial church. A few weeks later in another conversation the supervisor again became quite agitated. Again Carl simply tried to share his convictions. Sometime after this the supervisor invited Carl to a Negro church where a friend of his was preaching. Carl was shocked but he went with him, and went back again another time. Shortly after, the supervisor told Carl, 'When you're ready to paint those new walls in your remodeling job at your church let me know, I want to come and help paint.'

"Let's turn the coin around and look at a Negro. Mr. M had a bitter feeling in his heart for whites--the white man never did anything for him. Mrs. M became a Christian through one of the sisters in our church who lived two doors away. But when the membership question came up her husband said, 'No. I'll never have you become a member where there's a white person in the church.' One evening my wife and I were invited, along with Mrs. M, to a neighbor's home for Bible study. Suddenly one of the M children burst in shouting, 'Mother, you have to come right away!' She went home to find her baby had turned blue. Before she rushed the child to the hospital, we offered to pay the bill if she didn't happen to have the money and then she could repay it later. This gesture apparently spoke to Mr. M. By the next time I saw him he had taken his first steps toward Christian faith. I walked up to him and we talked together. The bridge was the love of Christ working through men, however imperfect."

Many Things to Many People

In the free verse at the beginning of this chapter, Peter Ediger suggested that the Mennonite Church in the city is many things. As more and more Mennonite Christians find themselves in the city, the "how" of becoming God's people emerges in varying ways. In London, Ontario, Mennonite Christians are making an impact on the city through a varied witness.

A simple, dignified billboard on a busy street reminds, "It is better to light one small candle than to curse the darkness." A fitting sign for the front of the London Rescue Mission. Established in 1951 by the Western Ontario Mennonite Conference, the 1964 operating budget of the mission indicates the strength of respect and support which the city feels toward it: Of a total budget of $55,000, $13,000 is provided by United Community Service funds, $39,000 from city welfare reimbursement, $3,000 by the Western Ontario Board, and $9,000 by individuals.

Under the capable leadership of Pastor Alvin Roth, the mission program includes many facets--adequate personal and medical records of men who come, a work program at the mission for those most promising for rehabilitation, counseling services, referral to many agencies. The recent establishment of Bethel House, a self-supporting rehabilitation home for alcoholics, is a promising development.

"We have to have enough love and self-understanding in our hearts and our congregations to overcome our fear of people who are different," commented Pastor Roth. One man who came to the mission in 1952 sensed this kind of love. Writing about his experience later, he said, "My mind weighed the matter. The pastor must be one of three things--a gullible fanatic, a convincing professor or he really did have an experience with a very real God. If the last be true, it would be well to pay close attention." Today the man is the assistant superintendent of the Mission.

In another corner of London, Mennonite students of several

branches are a part of the University of Western Ontario. A few students live at the center where the Arnold Gingrichs are house-parents; many more students find this home to be a center of warmth for themselves and their friends. The London Mennonite Student Fellowship sponsored its first fine arts weekend in 1965. Through discussion, concert, and worship, the students witnessed to the academic community which is their world.

Some sessions of the "Mennonites in Conversation with the Fine Arts" weekend were held at the Valleyview Mennonite Church, located in still another corner of the city. While some students, as well as some of the rescue mission personnel, are affiliated with this congregation, it has grown with a definite sense of its own particular mission. In the spring of 1962, after several years of meeting in a house, the small congregation moved to one of the growing edges of the city. The specific site was chosen because it was an unchurched area and because most of the members lived on that side of the city.

The new church building is surrounded by a typical suburban scene--one-family middle-class homes, with high-rise apartments filling some of the vacant blocks. The congregation has expended much energy in the past three years becoming familiar with their immediate community and trying to formulate goals and program for their life together geared to the community. To meet the needs of a wide range of interests, for example, the Sunday-school hour offers a choice of subject material for adults. One quarter there was a class on Trends in Protestant Thought and one on the Christian Home.

Mennonites as Catalysts

What is the "Mennonite image" in London, Ontario? Most Mennonite Christians there are not worrying about it--they are simply attempting to the best of their gifts, to be the people of God in their setting. A sociology professor at the university, having observed and worked with Mennonites in these London situations, suggested Mennonites are uniquely qualified to be a catalyst in mobilizing the resources of all churches of a city to work at particular human need. "You need to let your heritage work for

106

you," he said; "In contrast to many evangelical groups, you have a strong value system and a cultural background which gives stability."

The task and the challenge for Mennonites as an integral part of God's people is clear. In the hortatory style of the Book of Hebrews, Los Angeles Pastor LeRoy Bechler urges, "Let us lay aside the fear of the problem of our selves, and our way of life. Let us pray for divine power to make adjustments, to accept His love for all the city, the urbanized, industrialized, growing society, where we find the problems of public and private morality, of race relations and of family life which constitute opportunities of the first magnitude to us as Christians. Let us go boldly with His message. This will be the deciding factor if the city will be 'problem or potential' for us as a Christian Church."

To look at ways in which persons and congregations may become equipped for their Christian ministry in an urban world we now turn in chapter 8.

For Discussion

1. What lines from Peter Ediger's free verse could be used to describe your congregation?

2. Trace the rural strains in your community patterns. Reconstruct changes in attitude which have become apparent since 1940.

3. Evaluate J. Winfield Fretz's 1940 proposal to use mission funds to establish young people on farms. Might this have been a wise move at that time? Should it be considered right now?

4. How can we develop feelings toward the city which reflect today's situation honestly?

5. What evidences are there among Mennonites in your congregation and community that our heritage has provided some significant resources for bearing witness to Jesus Christ.

---

1. Ediger, Peter J., in *Mennonite Life*, Jan., 1964, pp. 3, 4.
2. Kreider, Robert, "Vocations of Swiss and South German Anabaptists" in *Mennonite Life*, Jan., 1953, pp. 38-42.
3. Peachey, Paul, *The Church in the City* (Newton: Faith and Life Press, 1963), pp. 68 ff.
4. Fretz, J. Winfield, "A Study of Mennonite Religious Institutions in Chicago" (unpublished BD thesis, University of Chicago, 1940) p. 12.

8 / Preparing for Witness

On a Sunday afternoon just before Christmas, 1956, Lee Heights Community Church held its first public meeting in the local grade school. In preparation for this day hundreds of homes had been visited. Invitations, letters, and reports had been mailed to people of the community. Pastor Vern Miller had been hard at work for several months. The response on the first Sunday afternoon was not overwhelming. Besides Vern and his family, there were *two* people present from the community. To make matters worse, even those two did not show up the following week! Vern kept on working and the Lord gave the increase. In less than 10 years the membership of this church has grown from zero to 156. Obviously things are on the move in Lee Heights.

Located about ten miles southeast of the public square in Cleveland, Ohio, the Lee Heights church serves a growing interracial community. In the heart of this suburban community, and situated along Lee Road, its main thoroughfare, these people erected an attractive new brick church building to serve their expanding fellowship.

But a growing membership and new buildings are not the most impressive things about Lee Heights. Rather, they are the changed lives and spiritual vitality that are to be found there.

A lady from the community said, "As we got acquainted with the Lee Heights church, I discovered that these people not only talked about their Christianity, they lived it. Many of the other churches," she said, "never get beyond the talking stage." Another middle-aged woman simply said, "This church is leaving a real

109

tentimony in this community." That sums it up pretty well. The points of attraction or initial contact are different for each individual. The methods are varied. But in any case, word is getting around in Lee Heights that lives are being changed over at the Lee Heights church. And so they are.

An example of how Christ is changing lives in this Cleveland suburb is found in the experience of Lloyd and Lessie Kenney. The Kenneys are most enthusiastic about their new life in Christ. Both now take joy in the work of the Lord, especially in pointing others around them to Christ. They never tire of telling neighbors and friends about their past life, how foolishly they lived, what it cost and "where we ended up." Everyone knows that their life at present is of a different order.

Lloyd works in an electrical products factory. "It was quite a thing," he recalled, "to make such a sudden change when the fellows all knew the kind of life I had lived before." But by God's grace he made the change. His new outlook was so evident that men on the job started calling him preacher. And today he often finds his fellow workers coming around for spiritual counsel and conversation. Explaining their missionary burden, Mrs. Kenney said, "Our responsibility is not only for those in foreign countries, but for those right here in our own backyard."

This kind of informal witness by Christians in their everyday life is now the chief means of outreach and growth at the Lee Heights church. Surprising as it may seem in a growing church like this, at present there are no organized visitation or evangelism "programs." In the early days at Lee Heights Vern Miller engaged in a rather extensive visitation and mailing program. But at the present time such contacts are left to the spontaneous initiative of members.

At the end of every Sunday morning message an invitation is given. Those responding to this weekly invitation make up a steady growth in the church and a month rarely goes by without the addition of someone to church fellowship. One comes home from a visit at Lee Heights, not primarily impressed by their program or organization, but rather with the memory of specific people and the warmth of their devotion to the work of the kingdom. [1]

110

*T*o be true to their heritage, Mennonites today belong in the city, particularly in the inner city. So spoke Franklin H. Littell to students at the Associated Mennonite Biblical Seminaries in 1961. "It seems to me," Littell said, "that as strange as it sounds in an address to a people that has been traditionally rural in orientation, the inner city is precisely the area which calls for the kind of community witness for which the sons and daughters of Menno are justly noted. In the world which we are moving toward, for some time to come the group witness to purity of life, Scriptural simplicity, nonviolence, sharing, spiritual government, the 'house church' as a community of brethren, etc., will be desperately needed.

"For generations the Mennonites have moved into the desert places and through faithfulness, mutual aid, and plain hard work turned prairies and jungles into garden places. What would be the impact if the Mennonites would tackle the most desperate deserts and jungles of America, the inner cities from which the prevailing forms of culture-religion are fleeting?" [2]

Heritage alone, however, is hardly adequate equipment to do the job which God is asking His people to tackle in megalopolis. Past achievement must be translated into present motivation. The record of our forefathers can provide direction for insights which may help us to face today's responsibility, but the transition from yesterday to tomorrow--from the no longer to the not yet--is a twentieth-century task. How then shall we prepare for the action to which God now calls?

Whether inner city or suburb the need and the response may be much the same. In each situation the challenge which confronts God's people is to sense both the blisters of need and the prescription for treatment. Most Christians, though, need help to understand the depth dimensions of modern metropolitan life. One attempt to begin pointing directions toward relevance is the Urban Training

111

Center in Chicago's West Side set up by twelve denominations, including the Mennonites.

A Center for Urban Training

Bifocal in emphasis, the Center weaves study with exposure in an attempt to help participants--both lay and clergy, both men and women--to broaden their metropolitan perspective. Attempting to develop creative ways for the church to carry out its mission the UTC experience centers around three tracks:

1. *Reflection upon the past*--the historical word and the historical event.

2. *Reflection and involvement in the present*--society with all its problems, complexities, ambiguities, fluidity.

3. *Reflection and involvement for developing future ministries of faithfulness*--doing the faithful servant deed and speaking the faithful prophetic word for our generation.

After a month at the Center in early 1965, O'Ray Graber, Mennonite pastor from Oklahoma City, emphasized, "The matter of being in the world but knowing ourselves to be men of faith, men of Christ, and reflecting upon what it means to be this kind of a man, or this kind of a fellowship, in the stream of life is taken very seriously."

John Braun, Waterloo, Ont., attended UTC four months after Graber, between his junior and middle years at Mennonite Biblical Seminary. Here is his candid appraisal. "In light of my June adventures, I'm somewhat disillusioned with my own denomination. What is the nature of the active gathered church in metropolis? It's a fellowship of believers. It's a lay movement, the traditional view of professional clergy is in question. It's a disciplined body. It's a congregation that has a keen social conscience and is sensitive to God's Word. It's a church whose social concern is based on the assumption that the faithful will always be in the minority. Are these all areas of familiarity? Don't they pounce out at us from our Anabaptist heritage? Why, then, aren't we at the helm of today's reformation to action?

John Braun's question probes deep. And his own words suggest at least one way to look for the answer. As we prepare for Christian

112

witness in an urban setting the several characteristics of Anabaptism which John pinpoints may well afford good clues: a believers' fellowship, a disciplined brotherhood, a servant community.

A Believers' Fellowship

Our forefathers were convinced that New Testament discipleship demanded mature commitment beginning with a thoroughgoing repentance. Repentance was a key word in some of the oldest liturgies for baptism--the symbol of being raised to new birth in Christ's resurrection the pledge of complete commitment to obey Christ. Anabaptist teaching asserted that the new birth, which must occur radically in both individual and the group, was the ground for integrity in working out a Christian witness. The preaching of the Gospel was an open invitation to any man to make personal absolution and covenant with God and His people. [3]

Response to the Gospel demands the same kind of repentance--of changing life direction--in the twentieth century as it did in the first or in the sixteenth centuries. Listen to Tom Gaines, a sound engineer and film producer in Lima, Ohio, as he recounts the spiritual pilgrimage of himself and his wife Carol.

"I was a skeptic and Carol a 'Christian' without any faith. We were a curious pair. I came from a home built on knowledge. Carol was in a church every Sunday up through her teens. However, her faith was not strong and it didn't take long for the scientific accent of a large secular university to reduce her beliefs to rubble.

"By the time Carol and I met and married, I had built barriers of prejudice against the tedious inconsistencies that I thought were the essence of Christian life and worship. After a few years, however, we began to admit to each other that life had more depth than dirty diapers and 30-second TV commercials. Together, slowly and quite uncertainly, we began to look for something.

"We attended churches. But Carol was skeptical because the answers they gave did not satisfy her. To make it worse, my university training was in logic, speech, and advertising . . . the preaching didn't get through my hypercritical defenses. Since the churches seemed to hold no answers to our questions of faith, Carol turned to the radio. Broadcasting was my profession at the time, and I was devoted to good content and quality programming. I turned a deaf ear to the Sunday morning lineup of religious broadcasts.

"However, one morning one of the programs stood out. It was *The Mennonite Hour*. As time progressed, we found encouragement in the messages--they made sense, were consistent, and seemed enthusiastic.

"Then one day Carol was introduced to a neighbor lady who it turned out was a Mennonite--the first we had met personally. Sensing Carol's spiritual hunger the lady asked Pastor Richard Martin to talk to Carol. His conviction and understanding brought Carol's faith back almost immediately. Carol thought that perhaps here was a preacher that even her prejudiced husband might tolerate listening to on a Sunday morning.

"I agreed to go to church with her. Together we found a group of Christians who knew their Bibles, and were enthusiastic about living its precepts. My defenses and criticisms drained away. It was only a matter of months before I followed Carol's steps and accepted Jesus Christ as my Lord."

The Gaines, now members of Salem Mennonite Church near Lima, are busy building a Christian home for their three young children. Jesus Christ has become the dynamic of their lives, both in homemaking for Carol and in film production for Tom. And they are growing in Christian faith. "There have been glorious times, and times of trial, but Jesus Christ has always been with us, and drawn us on in faith," Tom concluded. [4]

A Disciplined Brotherhood

Christian discipleship, although beginning with a personal call through the Gospel, is a call into fellowship--this our Anabaptist forebears made abundantly clear. In the judgment of Robert Friedmann, the central idea springing from the Anabaptists was "that one cannot find salvation without caring for his brother and that this 'brother' actually matters in the personal life." The way into the kingdom, the Anabaptists emphasized, was not by personal faith alone but by intimate brotherhood caring and sharing as commanded by Christ. [5]

A company of people in South Evanston, Illinois, are making diligent effort to translate this central tenet of faith into today's urban situation. This company, started in 1957, is known as Reba Place Fellowship, taking its name from a short street along which most of the members live. One of the things Reba Place Christians have been learning is what it means to "bear one another's burdens." Related to burden bearing as a weekly members' meeting from which emerge plans and decisions of the group. Here arrangements can be made to spend an evangelistic evening with neighbors, to send blankets to Algeria, or to adopt Korean orphans--as two families have done. Here gifts and schedules of various members can be reviewed and related to particular needs.

This process of prayer, admonition, and spiritual renewal is not an end in itself. The church does not engage in these disciplines so that her own company may be more congenial. Rather, it is for the sake of service in the world that the church prepares itself. Thus the task of the church is not to maintain a program but to function as a kind of workshop in Christian experience from which each member can go out to serve Christ in the world.

The people at Reba Place have let their relation to the church be decisive in making decisions about work and housing. Consequently, members all live within walking distance of one another, thus opening the door for developing a whole range of interrelationships which enrich fellowship. No church building, in the traditional sense, has been built. An ordinary house provides adequate space for meetings of the congregation (23 adults, 40 children, and guests). When the group gets too large for the house, persons are sent elsewhere. For instance, they commissioned one family to go to Atlanta, Georgia, in August, 1965.

Members of the fellowship are employed in factories, offices, schools, and hospitals throughout the city. Their pay checks are all deposited in a common church treasury. From this treasury the expenses of the church are met and each family receives a monthly budget for food and clothing. Whatever remains after meeting these immediate expenses is available for use in the work of the church wherever needed.

Some people have called Reba Place Fellowship an experiment

in communal living. To others it is known as a group that tries to practice honesty and confession. Others view its importance as an interracial housing experiment. Some think of it as a haven for emotionally disturbed persons. Others put it in the category of groups working for ecumenical Christianity. Each of these is but one facet of a larger reality, which, if taken by itself, is inadequate. The larger reality is a people seeking to "apprehend that for which they have been apprehended by Christ Jesus."[6]

A Servant Community

Followers of Christ preparing to bear faithful witness to their Lord recall that Jesus Christ came into the world as one who serves. In His person and in His ministry both the religious and the social dimensions of human life are inseparably combined. We who hear the good news are called to respond to the coming kingdom, to repent and abandon all other centers around which life can be ordered, and then to proclaim the Gospel to men outside its influence. But the proclamation is bound up with a commitment and community of life, planted in the midst of the world, whose primary witness is an existence rooted in the new kingdom.[7]

Christian witness, then, is double-barreled--to lead learners to become new persons in Jesus Christ, and to live as His servants in the world.[8] Jesus prayed to His Father that the disciples not be taken from the world. He wanted not escape but involvement, not withdrawal but identification. Disciples were meant for the marketplace, not the monastery; not to seek release from problems but answers to them. Paul N. Kraybill has observed, "We will never communicate to the men of our world who are trapped in frustration and cynicism unless we share deeply with them in personal encounter to the point where we ourselves feel something of the frustration and cynicism that tears at our own hearts. It is this giving up of ourselves into the suffering servant attitude which is the key to a new sense of witness in the world of today and tomorrow."[9]

Christ could do what He did because He became man incarnate. As Christ washed the feet of His disciples, so His followers seek to identify with whatever hurt or grievance or ill there may be

116

among the people whom God would reclaim. Witness is first and foremost *presence*; living *with* and caring *for* people--sharing joy as well as sorrow so that words will be backed by caring deeds. As our Lord suffered, so we will have to suffer; as suffering servants, we can reveal the Suffering Servant.

Although service has characterized much of Mennonite witness it should be noted that this mission of service has largely been carried out away from the local scene. As we now move from communities of rural comfort into the city, we have opportunity to center our mission in the very heart of unmet need. The ministry of service, coming along with or after the ministry of presence and before the ministry of verbal witness will have merit whomever Christians serve. [10]

The Evangelical Community Center in Saigon, Vietnam, according to missionary Luke Martin, is a place where a person can hear the good news without entering a church--it is an English school, a reading room, a nursery, a recreation center.

"We call it a community center because we wanted all age-groups to be attracted by the facilities and the activities. We wanted to relate to real community needs. We organized several English classes for students and adults. Many people wish to learn English, so we can fill a community need as we make friends in our classes. We opened a reading room with daily newspapers and magazines. Many students borrow English or Vietnamese books from the lending library. During mornings, 30 neighborhood four-to-six-year-olds come to kindergarten while their mother works. Sunday afternoon services provide a more formal opportunity to discuss questions of Christian faith, whereas the Tuesday evening Bible meeting is more informal.

"This is the Evangelical Community Center. It is a place for students to study, for children to play and hear Bible stories. It is where the staff must confess to one another, and pray for guidance as it seeks to bear witness to the Gospel of Christ. It is where neighborhood children try our patience by tearing down posters or picking fruit in the garden. It is where Mr. Tieng can raise serious questions about the Christian faith. It is where Mr. Khoa can share his fears of family disapproval if he believes in Christ. It is where Miss Qui is experiencing Christian community with youth and age, with American and Vietnamese: those who have committed themselves to Jesus Christ. It is where peace is proclaimed."

Preparing for witness today then, means that we take our heritage seriously but that we seek to translate that heritage into guides for the ordering of our present life together. The ideal way to prepare for witness is simply to *be* the kind of church which in reality is the church--a believers' fellowship, a disciplined brotherhood, a servant community. To consider how we may move toward increasing Christian involvement in an urban world through purposeful strategy we now turn in chapter 9.

For Discussion

1. Look seriously at Littell's question, "What would be the impact if the Mennonites would tackle the most desperate deserts and jungles of America, the inner city?"

2. Should Mennonites be sponsoring more students at the Urban Training Center? Would it be preferable to develop a distinctly Mennonite center?

3. In your own words, what should characterize believers, fellowship? A disciplined brotherhood? A servant community?

4. Evaluate the ministry of Reba Place Fellowship, particularly its economic discipline.

5. Does the Saigon Evangelical Community Center suggest any ideas for servanthood in your community?

---

1. Vogt, Virgil, "Emergent Church in Cleveland," in *Christian Living*, Oct., 1961, pp. 14 ff.
2. Littell, Franklin H., *A Tribute to Menno Simons* (Scottdale: Herald Press, 1961), p. 50.
3. Littell, Franklin H., *The Origins of Sectarian Protestantism* (New York: Macmillan, 1964), p. 84.
4. "I Was a Skeptic" in *Informer*, March, 1966.
5. Friedmann, Robert, "A Communication" in *Mennonite Quarterly Review*, April, 1944, p. 121.
6. Vogt, Virgil, "A Quest for Church Renewal" in *Christian Leader*, July, 1965.
7. Peachey, Paul, *Who Is My Neighbor?* (Newton: Faith and Life Press; 1964), p. 26.
8. McNeil, I. J., *Mission in Metropolis* (Grand Rapids: Eerdmans, 1965), p. 128.
9. Kraybill, Paul N., "How Do We Make the Message Relevant in Today's World?" in mimeographed proceedings of the Consultation on Theological Communication sponsored by the Mennonite Publishing House, Oct., 1964.
10. Franz, Delton, "Nature and Mission of the Church in the City" in *Mennonite Church in the City*, Oct., 1964.

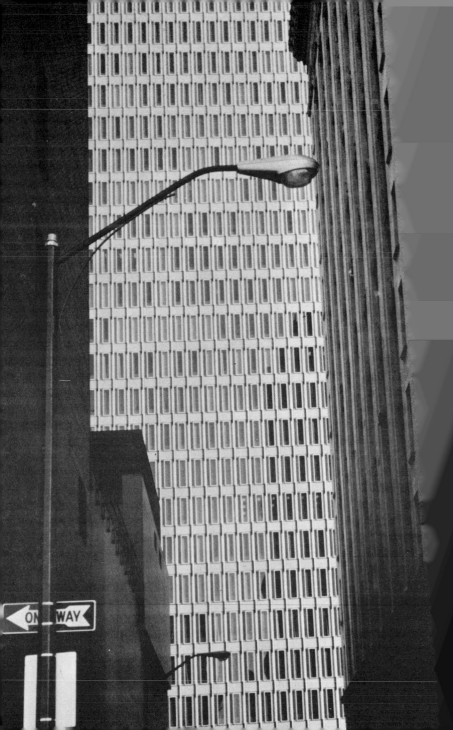

9 / Examining Future Direction

When the Rainbow Boulevard Mennonite Church (Kansas City, Kansas) was established, we frequently asked each other what our special contribution was in a city that had plenty of churches already. We have since learned to ask fewer self-centered questions, but have tried, rather, to discover our community.

After serving in outpost Bible schools, meeting for Bible study in the back of a drugstore, taking census, worshiping in a storefront church on Sunday evenings, conducting youth activities, and involving ourselves in neighborhood problems, we are beginning to learn the difference between being church-oriented and world-oriented in presenting Jesus Christ.

Not all of us in the congregation want to be community-oriented rather than church-oriented and we find ourselves continually helping each other adjust to a new situation. Coming from congregations that competed with PTA, Lions Club, or civic activities, and which tried to get members to withdraw from them, we encourage members to infiltrate such organizations and there share convictions. We endeavor to identify with the community, caring little about getting a bad name because of these associations.

Such activity carries with it a risk. We find we can't share our faith well, or that we have only customs and not much faith to share. We may even endorse, by our participation, actions we think are wrong, and find we have to share responsibility for many things we once blamed on others.

Attempting to present Christ in relevant ways has led us into the civil rights struggle, city government, organizing with neighborhood churches to attack problems cooperatively, and extensive work with poverty fund applications. We have painfully awakened to recognize our inability to witness easily and effectively outside the traditional Sunday service.

But our witness is more than a protest. We have tried to shepherd children, youth, families, and older people. Because we do our share of caring for the community, we have more right to help criticize and change it than if we stood aloof.

The road ahead is long, and we have only begun moving outward by taking a few steps away from our withdrawal and abandonment of the world. Our hope for the future is that we might be able to see what God is doing, not only in churches, but in the world and join Him more and more. [1]

"Be it resolved," delegates to the 1965 meeting of the Mennonite Board of Missions and Charities affirmed, "that we who represent the Mennonite Church in mission, renew our dedication to the task of being the church in urban areas." The resolution went on to explain that such dedication demands hearing the call to both inner city and affluent suburb, to both enlarging culture and knotty problems--into this complex context the Christian community is called to proclaim reconciliation. Like Rainbow Boulevard, many Mennonite congregations must assess their future in light of the urban reality of today.

Shortly after the annual mission board sessions, Yorifumi Yaguchi, a young Christian from Japan and a recent seminary graduate, went to Chicago for exposure to an American urban community before beginning his ministry in Japanese urban centers. Mr. Yaguchi summarized his Chicago encounter crisply, "More

122

Mennonite youth should live among the people of our cities. The church has a responsibility in the urban centers."

During his summer in Chicago Yaguchi taught summer Bible school at Englewood, visited Japanese families in Evanston, discussed the Bible with work campers at Bethel, preached at Lawndale, Lombard, and Community Chapel. All of which is to say that he got around; he was able to feel the heartbeat of Chicago without a stethoscope. His summary reflections, therefore, need to be taken seriously by North American Mennonites: Mennonites should come out of their ghettos and live in the world; Mennonites in the city have abundant opportunity to witness to the way of peace espoused by the sixteenth-century Anabaptists; Only a minority of Mennonites are really trying to communicate the Gospel; Rural Mennonites must be invited to the city to live and witness within the church community.

Purpose, Goals, and Strategy

"What might happen," *Missionary Messenger* editor Omar Eby has asked, "if a Spirit-directed, hard-nosed look were taken at an urban mission area and workers were made to discuss purposes and goals, and a five-year plan of strategy were drawn up?

"Could we bring ourselves to admit that we haven't any clearly defined long-term goals (that our sharpest concern is to keep VBS attendance up to the past five years' average), that we have been playing church? Could we even welcome the disruption new approaches would bring to our two-services-on-Sunday-and-a-midweek-Bible-study diet?"

Should God's people try to determine a strategy for extending the community of faith? Some persons fear that any attempt to devise a careful plan aimed toward specific goals will despiritualize the church, that strategy will tend to overemphasize human rather than divine factors in building the church. Area overseer E. M. Yost, Denver, Colorado, for instance, told us that the Mennonite outreach in Colorado is being determined by people, not by strategy!

Most thinking Christians, however, and unquestionably Overseer Yost would agree, recognize that careful consideration must be given to sensing what it is that God is seeking to do in His world through His people today. Church planning, according to one definition, is "that process whereby we assess the facts, the factors, the forces, and the future of society, in the light of the mission and purposes of the church, with a view to accomplishing these purposes effectively and efficiently." From this definition several principles of planning for Christian mission emerge.

1. Determine strategy by community need
2. Set both long-range and immediate goals
3. Plan comprehensively and cooperatively

These three general principles for charting Christian witness can be applied to any level of planning--congregational, community, conference, denominational, or world-wide. Because of the nature of our particular study, this chapter is designed primarily to help congregations think ahead--but always in light of their community, their denomination, and the world-wide Christian fellowship.

Determine Community Need

A local congregation seeking to fulfill its ministry in the world will soon discover the importance of understanding community organizations and being sensitive to their workings. When a congregation attempts to take concrete action on a specific human need it will immediately come into contact with other corporate structures. To help delinquent youth will usually require dealing with the police department, the courts, the school. Concern about unemployment will bring a congregation into cooperation or tension with the employment office, board of education, unions, corporations. Christians who think only in terms of individuals and ignore the reality and power of structures will be severely hampered in carrying out their mission.

A primary task of the local congregation is to inspire and train its members to carry out the mission of Christ in their world of work. A congregation can help its members to discover what their mission means in that context only if it has some knowledge of community issues. This means concern for the whole metropolis--facing outward towards the world rather than inward towards itself. Recall how the Rainbow Boulevard congregation shifted their

124

concern from introspection to neighborhood need. [2]

An important initial step in determining strategy is the asking of right questions. A guide prepared for use in Mennonite congregations suggests seven beginning questions.

1. Why does this congregation exist, and/or continue its existence in this locality?

2. To what extent does this congregation assume to carry responsibility for the community in which it is located, such as for the unchurched, for the moral tone of the community, for its schools, its recreation, its moral delinquencies?

3. To what extent does, or should, this congregation plan its program to serve its own people, or the people of the community, or both?

4. To what extent does, or should, the program of this congregation take into consideration, relate to, or cooperate with other Mennonite congregations, and congregations of other denominations in this community?

5. What general objectives are evident from the present congregational program?

6. To what extent, if any, would our program need to be changed if we really plan to carry out our "professed" objectives?

7. What goals, if any, have been set to help realize the objective of our congregation?

Questions focus important areas for discussion and action. Strategy for the people of God must be built on basic purposes and objectives. If a particular phase of congregational life is not achieving the need for which it was established, it must be altered until it does that which the congregation desires. Developing a strategy means that responsible people need to think through objectives, and then plan steps to work toward their goal.

Set Goals After Study

An Ohio suburban Mennonite congregation attempted a church life and mission self-study in mid-1964. From a membership questionnaire extensive data was assembled providing precise factual information as well as subjective feelings. Persons were requested to respond to questions such as:

125

- What do you feel are the strengths, assets, or drawing aspects of our congregation?
- What do you feel are weaknesses or gaps in our congregational life?
- What changes would you like to see?
- How large would you like our congregation to become?
- What role, function, and responsibility would you see our congregation having in the future of our community?
- What are some of the issues you think our congregation should and will face in the next ten years?
- How would you describe our congregation to a newcomer in the community?

At the same time the congregation divided into four work groups to study various facets of congregational life. Group 1 attempted to appraise the wealth base for congregational giving. Group 2 tried to determine where members lived in relation to the church building. Group 3 analyzed the history of the congregation to assess its past strengths and weaknesses, its effectiveness and ineffectiveness. Group 4 evaluated the needs of the present community and the changes anticipated in population and atmosphere.

On the basis of the completed questionnaires along with the reports of the four work groups, the Church Council brought to the congregation a summary report with recommendations for general directions, emphases, and possibilities for the future mission and ministry of the congregation.

Plan Comprehensively and Cooperatively

The idea of the congregation as the locus for mission has been pushed hard in the past decade or so. Alongside this emphasis we must begin to recognize that urban society is so complex that the whole people of God must move together. Since industrialization provides the style of thinking and the pattern for operating our urbanized way of living, the church must engage men in the large organizations as well as in the residential community. The main problems within the metropolis center in the places where human justice and dignity are at stake, where men's lives are being made or broken. Such issues transcend the boundaries of the residential neighborhood where the local congregation tends to focus its efforts. Automation, unemployment, retraining, welfare and relief, the changing requirements for education, research, and development, urban renewal, metropolitan planning-- these issues of life and death must be confronted by God's people.

Such confrontation means that the church needs to supplement its traditional congregational form with forms which engage men in urban structures--school boards, city councils, labor organizations. For years the church has sent pastors as chaplains to schools, hospitals, prisons. What is now needed is an expansion of this insight beyond institutions where persons are temporarily removed from normal life. The church must learn how to engage people *where they are*--in the mainstream of life's struggles and achievements. Engagement through specialized ministry can involve serious, searching conversation with Christian and non-Christian on the central issues with which the community's key institutions are concerned. Specialized ministry and congregational ministry can enrich each other. The specialized ministries can contribute to enlivening the preaching, teaching, and worship that take place in the congregation. The gathered congregation; on the other hand, can contribute Biblical insight and Christian motivation for developing a ministry on the job and in community responsibilities.

Furthermore, cooperation and communication between various segments of the whole church must mark the days ahead. Churches in the suburbs and in the inner city can strengthen and share with one another in their respective ministries. For example, two Chicago area congregations--Lombard and Woodlawn--are engaged at this writing in just such an experiment. After two sessions, several participants were asked whether the congregations should continue to dialogue. One spokesman replied, "Of course. We have just started to learn and to act together." Within a given region of the city, churches of different denominations, too, must work together if they are to meet the needs of men in their metropolitan area.

North American Christians need as well to work alongside their sister churches overseas. An Asian church leader asked Wilbert

127

Shenk a year ago whether the Mennonite Board of Missions could send someone from North America to help them prepare for witnessing in the cities. Year after year Asian young people are streaming from rural areas to the cities for education and to find employment. "I had to admit," Wilbert said, "that we in North America really have little more experience than they. Rather, I proposed that we should attack the problem together. I am convinced that it will be through practicing partnership in obedience to Christ's commission that we will discover the new avenues of witness."

The Dilemma of Church Planning

As part of an attempt to evaluate church effectiveness the National Council Bureau of Research and Survey has raised several significant questions:

1. Do local church members believe that they are acting in witness to God's personal call to them? Do they view their church as a form of Christian vocation?

2. Do church members believe they are members of the community whose sins are forgiven by God, reconciled with one another through Christ, and called by Christ in history to work together as His community in the world?

3. Do church members believe themselves to be reconciled with God and involved in helping in the work of reconciliation of God and world in sinful rebellion against Him?

Such questions begin to uncover the primary but more intangible dimensions of church reality. Although tangible factors which shape the church are important--numbers, buildings, finances, committees, and the like--we must finally know what it is that people experience in church. And it is here, as Paul Peachey, himself a trained sociologist, pointed out so pungently in *The Church in the City*, "we reach the crucial limits of sociological inquiry."

Peachey, in concluding his chapter on "City Church Research and Planning," questions the basic assumptions of the whole research-planning tradition. "If the church," he asks, "is perpetually constituted by the repenting, believing, and obeying

128

response of men to Christ, what precisely transpires when a building or an organization is set up by bureaucratic procedure without necessary reference to such a response? It would be presumptuous to propose single-handed answers to questions as enormous and universal as these. But they must be pressed home in a thousand ways until we can discern the answers that sound forth in the new community Christ would build even now in our midst."

For Study and Discussion

"Let's Look at Our Congregation" is planned to help congregations begin looking purposefully at themselves in light of their mission in the community and in the world. Questions in "Consider Some Basic Facts" should be assigned to individuals or small groups several weeks in advance of the session in which discussion and action is scheduled. "Take an Every-Member Opinion Poll" can be duplicated to use as an exercise during the session; participants should assign a number from 5 to 0 for each item depending upon their response to the question--5 would indicate an unqualified "yes," 0 an unqualified "no" and the numbers between would indicate "Partially."

1. Bohn, Pastor Stanley, in *Mennonite Church in the City*, July-August, 1965.
2. White, H. C., and Batchelder, R. C., "Mission to Metropolis" in *International Review of Missions*, April, 1965.

LET'S LOOK AT OUR CONGREGATION

Consider Some Basic Facts

1. *In what kind of a community are we located?* (its history; topography; socioeconomic situation including population composition --nationality, race, religion--and population trends; business and industry; educational resources; character-building and recreational agencies; social life; health facilities; social problems; political situation; civic, service and labor organizations; any other features creating special opportunities or problems)

2. *What is the history of our congregation?* (its beginnings; major developments and changes particularly as related to the world at large such as wars, depressions, migration, urbanization; outstanding events; outstanding personalities)

3. *What has been our membership growth?* (graph membership totals by five-year periods as far back as records are available)

4. *Where are our members located?* (spot membership on a map showing distance from the church building)

5. *What is our age and sex breakdown?* (construct a chart showing members and their families in age and sex groupings)

6. *What is our congregation's relation to other churches?* (list all churches in the community; briefly evaluate their ministry; describe the working relationship of the churches including any official overall cooperative organization or any specific project such as a community vacation Bible school)

7. *What is our congregation's relation to other community agencies?* (describe working relations with agencies such as schools, Red Cross, United Fund, the Y, community centers, Scouts)

Take an Every-Member Opinion Poll

1. Our congregation evidences evangelistic vision in its planning.
_____

2. Our congregational Life suggests evangelistic motivation.
_____

3. Our congregation maintains a responsibility file--names and addresses of persons not in obvious fellowship with Christ. _____

4. Our congregation has participated in a community census within the past three years, sponsored either by our congregation or by cooperating churches._____

5. Our congregation provides resources to stimulate evangelism and to help equip members for Christian witness in the community and beyond. _____

6. Members are encouraged to enter Voluntary Service and/or church-related service as an occupation. _____

7. Some members schedule regular evangelistic visits in community homes._____

8. Some members and/or our pastor visit shut-ins regularly. _____

9. Our pastor often emphasizes evangelism in sermons, and occasionally invites persons to make public decision for Christ. _____

10. Our congregation welcomes strangers and makes them feel at home. _____

11. Our congregation demonstrates warm Christian love toward persons whose backgrounds are different from ours._____

12. Children who are not yet baptized are made to feel that the congregation is interested in them as persons._____

13. Members know each other well and church membership is personally meaningful. _____

14. Our congregation attempts to have every member feel a natural part of the group._____

15. Our congregation has a wholesome attitude, and appreciation of, other Christians in our community._____

16. Most of our members carry some designated responsibility in our congregational life. _____

17. Our community is well informed concerning our congregation--what we believe, and how we translate that belief into life. _____

18. Our regular worship services are adequately planned to meet the needs of the congregation._____

19. Some of our services are planned to appeal to people in the community. _____

20. Our congregation has my enthusiastic support. _____

10 / Looking Toward the City of God

At its best moments, the Lombard Mennonite Church regards itself as composed of people called into being by God through Christ to be a responding channel for His creative activity in west suburban Chicago. With a present membership of 80 representing over a dozen religious backgrounds, we see one another as God's gifts and we see ourselves together as a people having gifts for ministries and witness outside the church walls. The congregation is regarded as a center for personal growth

where face to face groups minister to the searching, questing spirit through Biblical exploration;

where worship clarifies vision and renews resolution through celebration of the presence and saving actions of God;

where opportunities exist for facing the moral and spiritual issues of our time;

where family members both share and receive the gifts of the Spirit including those of sympathetic acceptance and assistance. Moreover, the congregation sees its role not only as a gathered but as a scattered fellowship with an unfinished task of witnessing love

in communicating the Way;

in being a social conscience;

in doing acts of service;

in serving on the front lines with our justing and redeeming God.

Preaching is an integral part of the weekly worship hour which is regarded as three services. The service of confession includes the celebration of God's presence, a hymn and prayers of adoration, confession, and thanksgiving. The service of the Word includes an anthem, the lessons--one from the Bible and one from another source, prayers of supplication and intercession, a second hymn, and the sermon, or witness to the Word--frequently by a lay person. The service of dedication includes a third hymn, the dedication of ourselves and our gifts, and the commissioning benediction.

What may be the most exciting venture of Sunday morning is the adult discussion labeled "Yes, but. . . ." Following worship, the discussion hour is an opportunity for persons to register questions, doubts, and insights with the subject fresh in mind. Through panels, discussion groups, reports and responses, directed study, and informal sharing, participants aim to clarify the topic, move toward group consensus, and finally make a commitment. For example, after discussion of civil rights, one couple felt constrained to travel to Selma, Alabama. They went as official representatives, sponsored by the Lombard congregation.

The first Sunday evening in each month is used to transact congregational business and to share inner disciplines--a program cultivating a deepening communion with God through voluntary daily disciplines of reading, meditating, and praying. Other Sunday evenings are given to special programs and elective studies such as the International Uniform Bible Lessons or selected current books like *Salty Christians*. Congregational life is planned by four commissions which meet on Wednesday evenings after choir practice: education, stewardship, fellowship, evangelism and service.

Currently we are seeking to understand what it means to be men of faith in today's world. Believing that a private faith is not to be privatized, that a man's most natural witness and ministry is in the sphere of what he does, that God in Christ is right now in the world reconciling principalities and powers, that churchmen are to go into this world rubbing elbows and in dialogue with others--believing this, we ask, "What two or three

134

vital needs exist in our community, in our nearest city, in our country, in our world?" These needs, viewed from the standpoint of both evangelism and social concern, chart the front lines of action.

The next question is, "What strategies will enable meeting those needs?" Different levels of joint as well as personal endeavor are recognized: inter-church Lombard, inter-church Chicago area, inter-church conference area, and denominational. Finally, we ask, "What disciplines will help us implement our strategy?" We have found the following helpful: financial covenanting, special problem seminars, Biblical, theological, cultural, education, discerning the times, sharing frontier concerns.

Newcomers to Lombard (names come via the water department) are sent a welcome brochure from the church. Lay members follow up the brochure with a telephone call to personalize the greeting. If they are not actively related to a local church, the newcomers receive a personal visit. One such newcomer was Don Zochert, 27, an overnight news editor for United Press International. Initially, the callers from the congregation were spurned at the Zochert home, but witnesses persisted. After Don's reception into Lombard Mennonite Church, the following note came to the pastor: "Just a brief note of thanks--it has been not only your unstinting friendliness, but your style of living that has helped us hear for the first time with any understanding the call 'Follow Me.' " In retrospect, Don attributes as the tools which the Spirit used in helping him to his new life the "openness and the friendliness of the pastor and congregation, and their whole body of concerns of what they say in the confrontation of the church with the world."

Don has helped us at Lombard see how we can serve as co-laborers with God in our occupational settings. Even in chess games on the 8:05 commuter, members have found those to whom they could relate redemptively. Our small membership has also found significant opportunities to express values and concerns in community tasks other than work.

After observing church life at Lombard Mennonite, seminary student Hong Won Kwon shared with the congregation this summary word, "I observed here a shared ministry." We believe, and aim to operate as though Paul's words concerning a shared ministry are true--"Each of us has been given his gift, his due portion of Christ's bounty" We continue to dream dreams of new gathered-scattered ventures in shared church ministries. As we dream, we move ahead sensing that whether in new ventures, or old ones tried anew, that continuous cyclic experience of gathering and scattering, worshiping and working, weekend and weekday is basic to our life together in the world. [1]

The failure of Babel's tower recorded in Genesis 11 is a parable of man's inability to build a stable secular civilization by himself. But at Pentecost, the language barrier which began at Babel was broken down and a new society was born--not because of what man achieved, but because God's mighty acts were proclaimed. Beginning with Pentecost, the Christian church--referred to commonly throughout the New Testament as the bride of Christ--calls men from every tribe and nation to be the people of God. In the final lines of the New Testament, John on Patmos records how he sees the holy city like a bride coming down from heaven and exclaims, "Now at last God has his dwelling among men! He will dwell among them and they shall be his people" (Rev. 21:3).

Until the day when the holy city descends, however, the crucial question we face is, What does it really mean to be the people of God today? This question has confronted the people of God in every generation and in every situation since the flub of Babel. To discern the answer means wrestling with the interrelated issues of church and world and mission under the lordship of Jesus Christ. Such wrestling, hopefully, has characterized our considerations in this study. Finally, though study must end. Discussion must give way to *being*, to *acting*, to *becoming*. George Webber said it succinctly in *God's Colony in Man's World*:

Christians are called by God to be and to act, not, endlessly to discuss.

Perhaps the essential problem in the life of the church today is her unwillingness to face realistically the fact that she may be bankrupt. We tend usually to search for yet another program gimmick as the answer to our bankruptcy in order to make our barrenness look respectable and our lack of reality appear to be what it is not. The church has not been willing to listen intently to what modern man is asking: I am lonely, who will love me? My life has no meaning, who will point me toward reality? Neither has the church been willing to listen seriously to what God is saying: Proclaim to every man that Christ has come to point the way toward life abundant.

Nothing Ever Happens in a Church

The church as modern man knows it usually gives him little reason to think that she has any superhuman resources to make any difference in a tangled world. Witness workshop conversations with men on the streets, according to Nelson E. Kauffman, reveal that most non-church goers question whether the church renders any positive effect today. The church just isn't speaking to real issues, they say. For example, in Vancouver, only 2 out of 15 persons interviewed had any kind of good words for the church. Such an attitude underscores the reaction of one of two boys wandering around the sidewalks in their inner city neighborhood.

"I'm going to throw a brick through that stained glass window," one chap threatened.

"You'd better not," the other said, "because that's a church."

"Aw, don't worry," retorted the first lad, "nothing will happen. Nothing ever happens in a church."

"In general," George Webber has summarized, "the picture is a bleak and discouraging one. The Protestant churches, aware of the problems, critical of their own failures, must now take far more realistically the concrete steps which obedience requires." [2] What are those concrete steps which obedience requires?

In Acts 2:42, Luke reports four distinguishing characteristics of the called together assembly of God's people. "And they devoted

137

themselves to the apostles' teaching and fellowship, to the breaking of bread and the prayers." In his preface to *These Are My People*, H. S. Bender said, "As I have sought to describe the church in its true being, I have had ever before me the vision of an identifiable, visible, human community, whose nature is determined by its response to the gift of God in Christ." Reponse in century twenty must entail radical dimensions. In what ways might God be asking His people to devote themselves to this fourfold discipline today?

Devoted to the Apostles' Teaching

The early Christian community shared common ideas based on common study of their spiritual forefathers. The Bible records God's acts throughout history. From Creation through the formation of God's people under Abraham, their liberation under Moses, their preparation for the Messiah, the divine plan finds fulfillment in Christ. His death and resurrection led to the outpouring of His Spirit. In this tradition then, guided by Word and Spirit, first-century Christians reflected on the apostles' teaching and lived in obedience to that reflection.

Our task today is to do the same. In her insightful book *The Witnessing Community*, the French Christian Suzanne de Dietrich wrote: Every generation, in communion with the long chain of witnesses who have preceded it and under the guidance of the same Spirit, must grasp anew the tasks that the Lord of the church sets before it. What the Bible offers is a vision of God's saving purpose for man and society. It presents us with an ongoing dialogue between God and His people. It is in listening to this dialogue, humbly, prayerfully, steadily, that God's Word spoken to other generations in other circumstances, will become a living Word to the men and women of *this* generation in *their* circumstances.

Bible study such as Miss de Dietrich describes means diligent discipline in an open, honest group setting. The traditional Sunday-school class can become the springboard for this kind of study. Participants in the King of Prussia, Pennsylvania, Mennonite Fellowship, for example, have found it so. "Our Sunday-school discussions are often the high point of our morning worship," Pastor John L. Ruth has reported. "We have sensed a freedom and searching spirit that has been encouraging. Christ's claim on us becomes vivid as we hear our brothers and sisters explain how the Bible affects their lives. As pastor I believe I can honestly say that I have never been in another group that came to grips so vigorously, week by week, with the message of the Gospel. We desire to be a fellowship in which the faith of our fathers is proclaimed in terms that will be understandable and relevant to our neighbors."

Devoted to the Apostles' Fellowship

Christian community does not just happen. It occurs when the gift of God's grace molds persons together to become a people not only with a common memory, but with a contemporary life meaningful to each other. The primitive church, according to the record, "were together and had all things in common; and they sold their possessions and goods and distributed them to all, as any had need" (Acts 2:44, 45).

Christian fellowhip is a focus of new relationships between God and man in Christ. It is a sharing of the apostles' teaching lived and proclaimed. It is created by God's presence in a redeemed humanity which exists for His worship service. As Gibson Winter has hinted in *The New Creation as Metropolis*, that the city for the church, is not only something to look forward to, but can be the setting for significant fellowship. "The testimony of God's people is that the New Creation to which they belong is at the same time, the source of their being and existence."

What is occurring in voluntary service units may point the way to deeper Christian fellowship in the context of congregational life. From VS leader Leroy Chupp in Portland, Oregon, came this word of witness: One of the outstanding experiences I enjoyed during the past four years of VS is the inter-relationship that breaks through when 15 searching young people, with their prejudices and ideals formed from different families, churches, and communities-- each with his own personality and concept of God and man--suddenly, like a shot out of a cannon, finds himself in the midst of a group. The joy and help that comes from living with a closely knit group of

Christians over a period of time can only do one thing--bring personal faith into an "active" stage, where a person is able to look beyond his own selfish little world full of pride, prejudice, and misunderstanding, into a world that is full of possibilities and responsibilities.

Devoted to the Breaking of Bread

"And day by day, attending the temple together and breaking bread in their homes, they partook of food with glad and generous hearts" (Acts 2:46). After the resurrection the disciples en route to Emmaus recognized their Lord when He broke bread with them. In the act of breaking bread, Christ has symbolized for His followers in every century the whole drama of salvation--in remembrance of a past event (Luke 22:19), in recognition of a present reality, in anticipation of the coming kingdom (I Corinthians 11:26).

But some commentators have noted that "the breaking of bread" refers not only to the symbolic meal but also to the fact that the meal was a source of real nourishment and an occasion of sharing substance. Devotion to apostolic fellowship means examining our finances as well as our spirit. While an economic discipline is less to the liking of American Christians than certain other disciplines, yet we must face our selfishness squarely in light of stewardship responsibility. As Mennonites we do well to consider with new seriousness both the liturgical and the economic aspects of the breaking of bread. Precisely what steps toward obedience should be taken remains for God's people in diligent fellowship to determine.

Menno Simons has described the essential communion fellowship in words which sum up the final qualities of the true people of God: Just as natural bread is made of many grains, pulverized by the mill, kneaded with water, and baked by the heat of the fire, so is the church of Christ made up of true believers, broken in their hearts with the mill of the divine Word, baptized with the water of the Holy Ghost, and with fire of pure, unfeigned love made into one body. Menno goes on to characterize the members of the body as friendly, peaceable, ever ready to serve by exhortation, by assisting--with deed, with possessions, with labor, with life--ready to forgive one another as Christ forgives and serves us with His Word, life, and death.[3]

Devoted to Prayer

Prayer was an underlying characteristic of the early church according to the Book of Acts. Prayer is part of the action of the Christian witness as he lifts his concern for his brother to God. Similarly, prayer has been found to be central in many renewing congregations today. The Maplewood Mennonite Church, Ft. Wayne, Indiana, experimented with a prayer group of six who devoted themselves to a ten-week discipline including weekly meetings coupled with daily personal prayer.

In reporting the experiment one participant wrote, "To pinpoint specific effects is difficult. One member confided that he draws great courage sharing his faith in his business life by knowing the rest of us are praying for him each day. Another expressed appreciation for the group as a clearing ground for radical ideas which he reads about and is anxious to discuss. Many times we church people struggle along in quite individualistic ways seeking growth in religious experience, only to discover that we are not too successful. We need the warmth and inspiration of others who are also forging in this area. I am convinced that prayer groups are a desirable means of helping some of us avoid disillusionment with the oftentimes heavy demands of organization, and of helping many to appreciate the real life and mission of the church."[4]

Along with small groups, some city congregations have discovered that a congregational retreat, away from the bustle of activity, provides occasional significance. In preparation for their 1965 annual all-church retreat, the Woodlawn Mennonite Church, Chicago, requested members to read Ephesians; to think about the questions, "What does it mean to be 'members of the body of Christ' and to be 'members one of another'?; and to use the membership roll as a prayer list, "asking for God's best for each person." Their congregational newssheet after detailing these preparatory disciplines, predicted, "May 29, 30 will be significant days for our church." They were.

How They Love Each Other

The quality of life which issued from the apostolic fellowship devoted to the fourfold discipline we have just discussed could best be summarized by a single but powerful word--love. Love was the authenticating quality which Christ encouraged His followers to emulate. Love was the characteristic to which the pagans pointed in derision when they described the Christian community. Writing near the close of the second century, Tertullian observed, "But it is the exercise of this sort of love which doth, with some, chiefly brand us with a mark of evil. 'See,' say they, 'how they love each other'; for they themselves hate each other."

Similarly, in a world seeking status and power through computers and missiles, it may just be that the task of the people of God is again to live out the radical way of love in real life. John W. Miller has reminded us that for most people in America today a Christian church is automatically assumed to involve a building, people meeting there on Sunday morning, and a clergyman in charge. "But Jesus had little or nothing to say about any of these three most prominent characteristics of the church in our time. He spoke instead of disciples loving one another. 'By this all men will know that you are my disciples, if you have *love* for one another.' "

For Discussion

1. Summarize and evaluate the congregational life at Lombard, both inside and outside the church building. What does "shared ministry" mean at Lombard?

2. Discuss the author's assertion, "The shape and style which mark our life together as Christians is determined too much by tradition and too little by radical faith."

3. Evaluate your own congregational life in terms of devotion to (a) the apostles' teaching; (b) the apostles' fellowship; (c) the breaking of bread; and (d) prayer.

4. What indications are there that twentieth-century Christians are known as people who love each other? What indications are there that they don't love?

5. What should be the mood of God's people today?

---

1. Kennel, Pastor LeRoy E., "New Ventures in Church Ministries," an address at Mennonite Biblical Seminary, Oct. 8, 1965.

2. Webber, George W., *The Congregation in Mission* (New York: Abingdon, 1964), p. 47.

3. Wenger, J. C., *Complete Writings of Menno Simons* (Scottdale: Herald Press, 1956), pp. 145, 146.

4. Naylor, Mrs. Ruth E., "Koinonia--And Me" in *Mennonite Church in the City*, May-June, 1965.